WHAT OTHERS ARE SAYING ABOUT
NOT LIKE ME

Not Like Me inspired me — a new follower of Jesus — to live the kind of life Jesus calls us to live. Jesus is the original diversity practitioner, who loves and welcomes all, and *Not Like Me* inspires us to follow his lead. Thank you, Eric, for reminding us to live this powerful and essential message.

JON GORDON, author of *The Energy Bus* and *Training Camp*

Eric Michael Bryant communicates a bridge-building message with grace and love. It is worth reading and definitely worth living.

DAVID ANDERSON, author of *Multicultural Ministry* and *Gracism*

Winsome, honest, theologically grounded, Bryant's work calls us to move beyond the theory of bridge building to everyday practical choices for actually loving others as Jesus loved.

NANCY BEACH, author of *An Hour on Sunday*

Not Like Me gets to the heart of our emotions to invoke in us the desire to be more like Jesus and to reach out to others, face our own selfishness, and be about Jesus' mission. Thanks, Eric, for this challenging book.

DAVE FERGUSON, lead pastor, Community Christian Church, Chicago, Illinois, and author of *The Big Idea*

God didn't design us to be rule followers. We were created to passionately love him and his creation — the wonderfully unique folks that God uses to interrupt our lives. In *Not Like Me*, Eric challenges us to engage that call. It's clever. It's fun. The book will force you to rethink your mission and your ministry. It will also leave you with minty-fresh breath.

TONY MORGAN,
author of *Killing Cockroaches and Other Scattered Musings on Leadership*

Authors ought to write with authenticity, and books ought to be enjoyable to read. This book is both. Eric Bryant is the real deal. And *Not Like Me* will challenge the way you think while putting a smile on your face.

MARK BATTERSON, lead pastor of National Community Church,
Washington, D.C., and author of *In a Pit with a Lion on a Snowy Day*

Eric writes with authenticity, humility, and passion. Using his own story of transformation as a starting point, he encourages and calls the church to demonstrate a love that is not blind but embracing. This book will move the church toward living with eyes and arms wide open.

MARY GLENN, training and partnership catalyst,
Kingdom Causes, Long Beach, California

Eric Bryant is a catalyst. He lives with reckless abandon in the constant pursuit of becoming more like Jesus and presenting a fresh expression of the gospel to those around him. In the pages of *Not Like Me*, you will experience what relational evangelism could, should, and does look like. A great read for leaders, young and old. Plan to walk away refreshed, energized, and equipped with new lenses through which to see the world, your community, and your friends.

BRAD LOMENICK, executive director, Catalyst, Atlanta, Georgia

Not Like Me is all about the heart and the how of evangelism. Bryant's style and substance reflect a refreshing departure from ineffective, shame-based witnessing techniques and a return to the simple and compelling compassion of Christ.

STEVEN FURTICK, lead pastor, Elevation Church,
Charlotte, North CAROLINA

This book could have also been called *Missional Living for Dummies*. It is a must-read for anyone who wishes to live for Jesus in urban post-Christian America.

DAVE BRUSKAS, campus pastor, Mars Hill Church,
Albuquerque, New Mexico

NOT

Eric
Michael
Bryant

LIKE
ME

A FIELD GUIDE for
INFLUENCING a DIVERSE WORLD

Formerly titled *Peppermint-Filled Piñatas*

 ZONDERVAN®

ZONDERVAN

Not Like Me
Copyright © 2010 by Eric Michael Bryant
Previously published as *Peppermint-Filled Piñatas*
Copyright © 2006 by Eric Michael Bryant

Requests for information should be addressed to:

Zondervan, 3900 *Sparks Drive SE, Grand Rapids, Michigan 49546*

Library of Congress Cataloging-in-Publication Data

Bryant, Eric Michael, 1972 –
    Not like me : a field guide for influencing a diverse world / Eric Michael Bryant.
      p. cm.
    Rev. ed. of: Peppermint-filled piñatas.
    Includes bibliographical references (p. 251).
    ISBN 978-0-310-32996-1 (softcover)
    1. Christianity and culture. 2. Multiculturalism — Religious aspects —
Christianity. I. Bryant, Eric Michael, 1972 – Peppermint-filled piñatas. II. Title.
BR115.C8B79   2010
    261 – dc22
                                               2010021293

Cover design: Jeff Gifford
Cover photography: Veer®
Interior design: Katherine Lloyd, The DESK

Printed in the United States of America

*For loving me
and teaching me how to love
For being my best friend
and allowing me into your world
For your patience and kindness
and allowing me to grow up with you
I dedicate this book and all I do to you, Debbie.
You are a living example of Proverbs 31.
For your gentle courage and being my best little buddy,
I dedicate this book to you, Caleb.
For your creative passion and being my beautiful little baby,
I dedicate this book to you, Trevi.*

CONTENTS

FOREWORD

Twenty-five years ago, we began our first cultural experiment in diversity. A handful of us committed ourselves to creating a place that did not simply welcome people different from ourselves but instead pursued them. It was a simple concept really: love knows no boundaries.

We were privileged to break down barriers that had for too long defined and maligned the church. As a Latin American, I knew all too well what it feels like to be the outsider. It is a strange thing to be invited into the kingdom but not always into the church. I also discovered that often, when invited into the church, the same opportunities for leadership were not afforded me as they were for others. I never put it in the category of racism or even prejudice; I simply accepted that all of us recognize the value of people similar to us more readily than the value of those who are different.

I have reluctantly accepted that after 9/11 I will spend my life as one who is subject to random search (especially when I don't shave), yet as quickly as I am now to be targeted for a pat down, I had been throughout my life as likely to have been overlooked for having leadership potential.

I am convinced that this is the leadership challenge for the twenty-first century: It is not whether we can embrace diversity or accept and love people who are different from us; it is whether we will be able to identify and reach the future leaders of the world.

The challenge we face is more than how to add some color to our churches. The future of our churches and the vitality of the movement of Jesus Christ hinge on this very issue. Christianity's credibility rests on the church's resolve to not only embrace the differences in people but to celebrate and unleash them.

For the last fifteen years, we have been a part of a community that has come to be known as Mosaic. Mosaic is a tribe of over eighty nationalities that have converged in the city of Los Angeles. In a city known for racial and ethnic polarization, something beautiful — something miraculous — has transpired. The city that inspired the Academy Award – winning film Crash has within her womb the birth of hope for its masses. It was here that Rodney King asked, "Can't we all just get along?"

Eric Michael Bryant answers this question; and what's more, he tells us how we can make it happen. And he isn't speaking from theory but from practice. Eric is an anomaly at Mosaic. He's a very white — and I mean very, very white — bald guy! If there ever would have been the experience of reverse discrimination, it would have been here. Yet no one has exhibited more cross-cultural dexterity and adaptation than he has. This capacity, as well as his uncanny leadership gifts, has positioned him to serve on our navigator team with me over the past several years. Eric has been an incredible gift to me and to Mosaic and the kingdom at large. His leadership and influence are invaluable not only to us here in LA; they reach across the world.

Here at Mosaic we give our leadership team superhero names.

Eric's is "Stealth" — our attempt to describe his unique ability to lead without being seen. Eric is a master of invisible leadership. He has learned the true art of leading leaders. This gift mix informs his writings and makes his contribution even more significant. Eric knows what he's talking about, and he practices what he preaches. He has been writing this book for several years; I'm just glad he finally wrote it down.

Not Like Me is *Saving Private Ryan* meets *Nacho Libre*! Eric calls us to a heroic mission and at the same time exposes our flawed humanity. He tackles one of the most critical and complex issues of our time and brings it down to earth and keeps us grounded in reality. It's quite a gift to force us to face such uncomfortable and serious issues and at the same time to keep us laughing. Somebody needed to write this book; I am grateful that Eric did. We will all be better as a result.

Thank you, Eric, for awakening in us a love that knows no boundaries.

Erwin Raphael McManus

Erwin serves as the primary communicator and cultural architect of Mosaic in Los Angeles. He is the author of *The Barbarian Way, Chasing Daylight,* and several other books.
Architect, *www.Mosaic.org*
Activist, *www.AwakenHumanity.org*
Innovator, *www.McManusStudios.com*

THE ART OF WOO

Overcoming the Christian Stereotype

I have a confession to make: I am a bald white guy (BWG) living in a world of color. It was not always this way, as I used to have hair and I used to live in the suburbs in Texas. While I had a great childhood and hope to provide my kids a similar kind of life, I realize that the world they are experiencing is very different from the world I knew growing up. Los Angeles in the new millennium and suburban Dallas/ Fort Worth, Texas, in the 1980s are in the same country but not quite the same universe. The world is changing dramatically, and as a result, we cannot live the same way, hiding in our own cul-de-sacs, staying away from others who look or believe differently from the way we look or believe, because now they live next door.

Living in Los Angeles as a BWG has opened my eyes to how others who may not look like everyone else must feel. I don't feel I look unusual. Sure, I know it's odd to be bald in my early thirties. It was even stranger to be losing hair in high school. (In fact, the one actual bald kid in our high school approached me one day and whispered in my ear, "Stop using your hair dryer." I should have realized that when someone who is follicly challenged gives you hair-care advice, you should immediately contact Rogaine.)

In the late 1990s, while I was working as the youth pastor at Mosaic in East Los Angeles, I was often confused with either a "cholo" (the shaved-head gangsters of East LA) or a skinhead (some sort of neo-Nazi). Of course, neither was true, and I despised the assumptions others made about me just because of my appearance. To eliminate any confusion, I avoided wearing bandannas, superbaggy pants, and swastikas. One teen made me feel a little better, but still a bit odd, as he offered to shine my head for a quarter every time I saw him.

Ironically, I probably wouldn't be bald today if I wasn't a Christian. Sounds funny, but it's true. At the very least, I know I wouldn't have gone bald so quickly. One of our youth workers encouraged me to offer to shave my head if the youth group brought seventy-five kids to an upcoming event.

Now, working with teens in a church requires one to make great sacrifices, one of which is dignity. I honestly don't know why youth groups across the nation seem to enjoy shaming their youth leaders. In an effort to coerce teens to come to events, youth leaders have been known to dye their hair, eat pig snouts, and wear adult diapers, among various other humiliating experiences. I don't remember Jesus offering such ridiculous incentives, but I suppose if we could walk on water or feed five thousand people spontaneously, we probably wouldn't be resorting to such crazy attempts to get the attention of our teens.

Seventy-five kids were fifty more than we averaged, so I thought I would be safe. I'm not sure why seeing me get my head shaved was more motivational than reaching out to their friends with the life-changing message of Jesus, but seventy-eight teenagers showed up that night.

With the razor humming, they shaved my head as everyone in the crowd screamed with delight — that is, everyone except my wife, Debbie, who feared my hair wouldn't grow back. Ridiculous thought, huh? Perhaps we should consider Debbie a prophetess, for her prediction came true. Angry with me for agreeing to such a foolish dare, my already-thinning hair refused to return. The recession had turned into a complete retreat.

But at least bald is a cool look. It *is* still cool to be bald, right?

CHANGING VIEWS

Growing up in the Bible Belt gave me a unique perspective on life. I haven't lived in the South since 1994, but since I spent most of my school years there, I feel I have some insider knowledge of Christian culture.

Perhaps things have changed, but when I was there, everyone claimed to be a Christian. For the most part, the white Anglo-Saxon Protestant worldview shaped the culture. In many ways I enjoyed and benefited from this environment growing up. Many amazing people influenced me and helped guide me spiritually. Even in public schools we would celebrate Christmas and Easter, while staying away from Halloween. We learned a great deal about the world in which we lived from a Christian and Western perspective.

Unfortunately, since *everyone* seemed to be a Christian, I discovered that for many, their faith remained more cultural than real. They cheered for the Dallas Cowboys, went out to eat at Chili's, and attended church because that's what Texans do. After seeing friends struggle through life-altering situations and decisions, I saw a genuine disconnect between what people said they believed and how they lived. Since the cultural peer pressure remained so strong, these struggles remained private, driving them further and further from the people who could help them, such as their parents or church leaders. Either those struggling felt judged by those around them, or the cultural pressure to be "good Christians" kept them from becoming authentic and vulnerable.

While attending Baylor University, I developed friendships with young men and women who seemed to have moved beyond this framework. They longed to change the world as followers of Christ who saw their mission field as the hospitals, schools, businesses, firms, or organizations in which they planned to work. I had always thought that Christians were supposed to stop sinning and attend church, so they could then donate money to the pastor so he could lead people into a relationship with God. Some of these radical college students I met actually wanted to be a part of serving others *personally* rather than paying someone else to do it. They wanted to contribute, participate, and even lead the charge. As I watched some of my friends start churches, businesses, ministries, and nonprofit mission organizations, I looked for my own place to risk and to sacrifice.

Their enthusiasm inspired me and ultimately changed the course of my life. My ultimate goal for college was to earn a degree so I could get a job, get married, buy a house, and raise my kids in a safe, comfortable, and Christian environment, but my experiences caused me to change this goal. When I began helping at a boys' home for kids in foster care and later worked as a youth pastor at a church that included primarily Anglo senior citizens in a diverse and transitional neighborhood, I had the opportunity to meet people who were overlooked far too often. In a sense, I realized that I had experienced so much love from God and from my family, friends, and teachers that I wanted to share this love with others. There were times I felt guilty for what I had, but this short-term motivation was replaced by gratitude. The love I had received fueled me to give to others.

My eyes have been opened to a very different reality from my suburban childhood as I have traveled outside of the Bible Belt. Whether I was serving in an economically challenged neighborhood in Brazil or on a mission trip in Mexico, helping to plant a church in Seattle, traveling to Europe to consider serving the immigrants from the Muslim world, moving to Los Angeles to volunteer at a church called Mosaic, or traveling to Egypt, Lebanon, Syria, Turkey, or Malaysia, I encountered people who not only did not pretend to be Christians; they, in fact, hated Christians. Conversations with Christian leaders from around the world have confirmed that a negative Christian stereotype was prevalent and spreading.

THE CHRISTIAN STEREOTYPE

We all encounter assumptions based on the stereotypes others have of us. People have preconceived ideas about us based on our appearance, skin tone, gender, choice in clothing, background, behavior, and even beliefs — and, of course, if we are honest, we make assumptions about others as well. Just as being a BWG in LA has created some challenges and even closed some doors, those of us who call ourselves Christians face the daunting task of overcoming others' perceptions of us in a world that sees us in a less than positive way.

With our religious heritage as a nation, "in God we trust" on our coins, "one nation under God" in our pledge, Christians have seen the United States as a nation filled with "good" Christians and "bad" Christians, unaware of the growing number of Muslims, Buddhists, Taoists, animists, atheists, cultists, and Hindus now living in the United States. I am not simply referring to those who move here from other countries, bringing their religions with them, although there are a lot of people who fit this description. I am also referring to the Christians who have walked away from the religion of their parents or grandparents to adopt a new way of seeing the world. More and more people see Christianity as part of their past rather than as a guiding force for their future.

The fading influence of Christianity is not unique to the United States. In the last century, Europe, Canada, Australia, and New Zealand, among other nations, have experienced a decline in the number of people interested in participating in a church. In the last twenty years or so, South Korea's enormous churches have begun to dwindle in size as young people have stopped going. How has this happened? How could "Christian" nations find themselves so rapidly and radically reshaped? Sure, there are glimpses of great things happening around the world — places where new churches are springing up and reaching new people in Africa, Latin America, Asia, and even pockets of the Middle East. And if we look closely enough, we can also see good things happening in the Western world. But why does it seem that so many are rejecting Christianity and wanting nothing to do with Christians while maintaining a high level of respect for Jesus?

More and more people seem to have the same attitude as the

bumper sticker I see on cars around town: "Jesus, protect me from your followers." Who is to blame for this anti-Christian bias? Is it the media? Is there a liberal conspiracy? Is it Arianna Huffington or Al Franken? Perhaps we can place the blame on the Supreme Court's putting an end to mandatory prayer in public schools in 1962, or making abortion legal in 1972, or allowing too many immigrants into the country in the previous decade or so.

In reality, if we are completely honest, many of us who call ourselves Christians are to blame. We have created an environment where we are seen as judgmental, irrelevant, mean, and hypocritical.

Sure, the gospel is a challenging message to share, but it is not the gospel that is turning people away from church. Most people don't like to be called sinful or to be told their eternal destiny won't be fun-filled, but typically our actions rather than our convictions have created this negative stereotype. I have met many people who have walked away from the church of their childhood in order to find "freedom." After years in youth ministry, I have learned from other youth leaders and discovered for myself the challenge of keeping teenagers connected to church after they graduate from high school. If we added up the number of people who stopped believing in God because they stopped enjoying church when they were in junior high or even twelve years old or younger, we would be shocked at how many walk away from the faith of their parents.

I can relate to the kid who finds himself forced to go to a place he does not enjoy. In my younger days, there were times I would sneak away from the church building to jump on a neighbor's trampoline. Other times I would fake an illness on Sunday morning to avoid going to church because of the boring music and boring sermons. Miraculously, when I was seventeen, I encountered God personally as I sensed Jesus inviting me to fully trust him with my life, yet the church was still something I had to endure, one of the sacrifices God was calling me to make. There were moments when I caught glimpses of what could be, especially at camp or in college, but the weekly routine remained less than inspiring.

After graduating from college, I traveled the world and moved to Seattle and then to Los Angeles in search of churches that acknowledged and addressed our ever-changing world. In my limited search, I discovered that there are no perfect churches, but there certainly are communities of faith that are expressing the eternal truth of God in ways that can be understood in our new world. Sadly, these communities seem to be the exception rather than the rule.

Many times, what we Christians perceive as persecution from the world is actually the direct result of our own mindless or even evil decisions. For one, we have a sordid past. In the name of Christianity, people have destroyed civilizations and forced conversions. The Crusades, the Spanish Inquisition, the "civilizing" of North America, and our participation in slavery don't look good on our résumé as Christians. Like you, I don't claim that these parts of Christian history are based on God's love and his principles, but I cannot help wondering what we are currently doing or not doing that will cause us to feel ashamed in the future.

For far too long, the world has been made aware of what we as Christians hate rather than whom we love. When asked what Christians believe, most people would begin creating a "Don't Do" list. People are far more aware of what Christians are against than of what we support. Rather than hearing a call for true freedom, people feel unloved by Christians and therefore unloved by God because of our behavior.

We tend to judge people who do not know Christ by the same standards we have for ourselves. We should not be surprised when people who have not surrendered their lives to God live differently. If we struggle to measure up to our high standards with God's help and intervention in our lives, how can we possibly have the same expectations for others who have not sought or received God's forgiveness and strength? It's like getting mad at Stevie Wonder for not waving at us when we walk past him.

Our personal relationships often betray our feelings for the world as well. Rather than befriending and loving those who do not yet follow Christ, it seems that the longer we follow Christ, the fewer people we actually know who believe differently from the way we believe. We have created our own world within a world, a bubble in which we live with everything we need: Christian books, Christian shirts, Christian music, Christian jewelry, Christian movies, Christian sports leagues, Christian stores, Christian video games, and even Christian mints. I'm all for entrepreneurial ventures, but I'm afraid we have (inadvertently or perhaps sometimes purposely) isolated ourselves from the world around us. Perhaps there are some who have been reached by reading a T-shirt with "God's Gym" on the front, finding a gospel tract on a urinal, or attending events featuring Christian bands, but most of the time we forget the importance of reaching out to others through these experiences. Instead, we choose to enjoy these events as an alternate reality outside of the rest of culture.

Some of our churches have so consistently become a refuge for Christians from the world that we fail to become communities that go out into the world, or even communities where seekers feel free to come and explore the possibility of a God who loves them and has a plan for their lives. We've even created our own language that now requires translation: Christianese. Our isolation from the world fails to communicate God's concern for those around us but instead communicates that we do not want others in our lives who do not know Christ.

In conversations with people who have rejected Christianity, many times they have mentioned racism, conflict, hypocrisy, and even a lack of compassion as key reasons. For years, we've all heard that the eleven o'clock hour on Sunday mornings is "the most segregated hour of the week," yet what have we done to change this? When the world sees us fighting among ourselves with church splits or hears of another pastor who embezzled money or left his wife, we just prove to them that we have nothing more to offer than what they are already experiencing. When non-Christians are moved to help those who are underprivileged, they volunteer at Goodwill or at a downtown mission. Serving the community rarely equates in people's minds with volunteering with a church. Too few of us are engaging the very real needs we should be meeting while inviting our spiritually open friends, family members, coworkers, and neighbors to join us.

THE ART OF WOO

If you are anything like me, you have moments when you dream of overcoming the Christian stereotype.

Deep down, we long to be part of a loving and diverse community. We long to be part of a church known for caring for those the world has forgotten. We want to live out our lives of faith in ways that would please God and intrigue those around us. Wouldn't it be amazing if people saw our lives and wanted what we have? Wouldn't it be tremendous if people saw us living by faith, expressing love, and sharing hope?

Rather than coming across as judgmental, homogenous, isolated, conflict-filled, and irrelevant communities, we need to show the world what Christ truly intended us to be. We need to practice what I like to call "the art of woo." In the sixth century BC, Sun Tzu taught us how to destroy others in *The Art of War*.[1] Someone else has taught us how to manipulate people in *The Art of Seduction*, so why can't we learn "the art of woo"?[2] I love The Gallup Organization's definition of woo: "winning others over."[3] The more common definition implies a romantic pursuit, one's attempts to gain the affection of another person. Both descriptions are helpful for us in this journey. We need more woo. Since we are God's children and representatives, those around us need to feel loved by us.

My hope is that these pages will inspire us to develop "the art of woo" so that we might learn to develop diverse communities, resolve conflict, overcome bitterness, create a better future, and even heal our fractured world. Wouldn't it be amazing if as followers of Christ we found ourselves as part of the solution in our divided world rather than as part of the problem? In the end, don't people matter most?

Signs of change are all around us. I am meeting more and more leaders who are determined to create communities that show and share Christ's love in fresh ways in their cities. These leaders and communities have inspired me to believe in a new future.

In addition, serving at Mosaic in Los Angeles has been a life-changing experience. Whether volunteering in the parking lot, hosting a small group, working with teenagers or college students, or serving as part of the leadership team, I'm continually amazed by this community. There are so many loving, sacrificial, talented, and courageous people, and we are all from such varied backgrounds. Not only are we diverse ethnically; we are diverse socioeconomically, generationally, politically, and even spiritually. Stepping into this diverse community as outsiders in 1998, Debbie and I immediately felt welcomed and included. For the last several years, I have learned a great deal from our community and our leaders.

My desire is to live a life that embraces the people Christians love to hate. I want to gain influence among those who look different, act differently, live differently, and believe differently. I want to overcome the Christian stereotype with love. I want those around me — whether or not they have a similar background and world-view — to be aware of God's love through my words and my actions. I want to take Jesus seriously when he challenged us to love God and love our neighbor. I want to learn "the art of woo."

This book is for those who want to join me and break the fourth wall. Too often, we live our lives as if we are on a stage. We want others to hear what we have to say and to watch us from afar. It's as if the message of Jesus has come just to us rather than through us and into the lives of those around us. When an actor in a play looks at the audience, talks to the audience, and listens to the audience, he removes an invisible barrier — the fourth wall. They are no longer the audience; they are now part of the story.

The journey won't be easy. If you are anything like me, you seem to fail more often than you succeed. We will disappoint ourselves at times. Furthermore, actually reaching out to people and loving them can be painful and heartbreaking. In fact, there are people all over the world who are being genuinely persecuted, imprisoned, and even killed as they try to love those who do not want their love. It is far easier to remain isolated and spend time with those who already love us, but there are so many others who need to feel and experience authentic friendship.

We live in a diverse world filled with unprecedented opportunity. No matter what your background may be, we live at a time in history when we have to learn to live among people who are not like us. Now is the time for us to become agents of change creating genuine unity among people from a variety of backgrounds and worldviews. Through stories and insights gleaned from my own experiences and failures, the experiences of others, and the life and teachings of Jesus, my hope is that we will discover how to move beyond ethnic, racial, cultural, and ideological barriers toward genuine friendship with others.

Part
1

PEOPLE MATTER MOST

■ Chapter 1

CURRY FAVOR

Winning People and Influencing Friends

Every Fourth of July, we celebrate the birthday of the United States with friends from church. Soccer, volleyball, music, and food at the park create a great environment to invite other friends who aren't yet connected to a church. A few years back, a friend of mine named Masayoshi joined us.

Erwin McManus, the lead pastor of Mosaic, and his family had just returned from time in New Zealand, so they were eager to share with us their newfound interest in the game of rugby. Masayoshi chose not to play, so I mentioned I would find him later. I love competition of any type, but the prospect of another type of football without pads fascinated me.

Even though Erwin explained the rules, chaos ensued after the kickoff. The twenty guys on the field kept reverting to North

American football rules. Rather than pitching it backward, we insisted on throwing it forward. We kept trying to block, tackle, and pass rather than ruck, maul, or scrum. In the end, as every single play ended up with several illegal moves, our enthusiasm began to die down, not to mention that we were becoming exhausted. I decided to take a break and find Masayoshi rather than trying to figure out the real rules.

I was hoping to get to know my friend a bit more. He had moved from Japan to study at Cal State University, Los Angeles, a school within walking distance of my house. Several people from Mosaic met Masayoshi, and he soon got involved with several small groups over the years. During this particular summer, Masayoshi participated in our backyard group and seemed very intrigued by our conversations. Even when he moved farther away, he faithfully came each week.

As Masayoshi and I sat in the shade, I asked him about his spiritual journey. He described how his background of growing up in Japan had influenced him toward a more secular way of looking at the world, yet with a deep respect for ancestors, connected to a mixture of Buddhism and Shintoism. Once he was in LA, a group of international students invited him to join them for weekly dinners. Not knowing anyone in the United States, he jumped at the opportunity to develop friendships. When he discovered that those hosting the parties followed Christ, he became more intrigued rather than turned off. He wondered why these strangers were so kind and seemed to genuinely care for him. He couldn't figure out why they seemed so happy and even intentional with their lives. As he continued to get to know more and more people who followed Christ, eventually he could not rationalize away what was happening in his heart. He decided to follow Christ too.

I was stunned. People in Japan have historically been quite closed to the idea of a relationship with Jesus. Yet for Masayoshi, after just a couple of years, he desired to entrust his entire life and future to Christ. At the picnic, he shared about his fear of his parents' reaction to this news. In order to honor them, he had decided to tell them about his decision on his next trip home, which was quickly approaching. With their blessing, he wanted to be baptized when he returned to Los Angeles.

Later that fall, Masayoshi was baptized, and after graduating, he eagerly looked forward to returning to Japan so that he might be able to help his friends and family discover what he has found in a relationship with Christ. His courage and resolve inspire me. I have often thought about how Masayoshi's life was so dramatically changed as a result of the friends he met in LA.

Compare Masayoshi's story with the story of a missionary family who lived for seven years in Japan without ever seeing a conversion. When asked if they had any friends, they responded with only the names of a few other missionaries. Sadly, they did not have any friends in Japan who did not follow Christ. This missionary family had a passion for reaching people. They studied outreach strategies in seminary and language school so that they could communicate. They had learned how to debate with Buddhists, Shintoists, and secular atheists, but they didn't know how to befriend them.

The missionary family spent years preparing for ministry in Japan and years in ministry in Japan, but they were playing the wrong game — just as in that rugby game we weren't just playing by the wrong rules; we weren't even playing the right game. North American football and rugby may be similar, yet they are worlds apart. We can't just tweak the pass here and the pitch there. The points are different. Defense and offense are different. There are no huddles in rugby. Once we stop trying to play football with a rugby ball, we will begin to enjoy the nuances of an entirely different game.

As followers of Christ trying to reach people, we are in a totally new game. We try to make minor adjustments to the rules, thinking that doing so will help us succeed, but we won't be able to break through until we start playing the right game.

Many of our programs, ministries, and churches operate as though our world is filled with people who want to be Christian and just don't know how. There is less interest in switching religions than we would even care to discover. Rather than simply looking for ways to develop new strategies and programs, we must hone the skill of developing relationships. We need to go back to the beginning and capture the essence of interaction with the world around us. Our future depends on recapturing our ancient past.

CURRYING FAVOR

The most effective apologetic is love. This may seem simplistic or even naive in a pluralistic, universalistic, spiritually heightened, anti-Christian, and syncretistic world, but knowing all the "right" answers is not nearly as effective as demonstrating a transformed life of genuine love and concern and care. We need to follow the apostle Paul's guidance to "preach the word; be prepared in season and out of season; correct, rebuke and encourage," while ensuring that we follow how he wanted his church-planting protégé, Timothy, to do this — "with great patience and careful instruction" (2 Timothy 4:2). As a college student preparing to preach the word and teach the truth, I began to discover through relationships with people who did not follow Christ that what I knew was not nearly as important as how I treated them.

As we shape the future of how we live our lives as followers of Christ, we need to look back at the beginning of our history. In a time and place in history when following Christ was considered a cult, even still the first followers of Christ were well respected among the people. In Acts 2:47 Luke describes these early followers of Christ as "enjoying the favor of all the people."

How is this possible? The customs and practices of this new understanding from God called "the Way" seemed absurd, ridiculous, or even offensive to those around them. Some had walked away from Jesus, thinking that he was advocating cannibalism as he referred to what we now call "the Lord's Supper" (see John 6:35 – 58). The idea that slaves and women deserved respect and honor seemed absurd and even revolutionary. These early Christians spoke often of death — personally dying to self, the martyrdom of some in their community, and the death of the Messiah on the cross. More radically, the men and women who met together daily to study the Scriptures and to serve others claimed that the Messiah had died, had miraculously rose from the dead, and now was mystically communicating with them through the Holy Spirit. I can guarantee, the early Christians weren't following the advice of Dale Carnegie and "winning friends and influencing people" as a result of their beliefs — so what was it? Perhaps they were reversing Carnegie's mantra. Could it be that the early Christians were "winning people and influencing friends"? Developing friendships takes longer and requires more effort, but the impact is greater and longer lasting.

To curry favor, the early followers of Christ had relationships with people who did not yet know Christ. Their message was one of tremendous hope, and they demonstrated sacrificial love. Sound simple? If you are anything like me, you know that what may sound simple to accomplish is actually extremely difficult to do.

We struggle to have friendships with those who do not follow Christ and even with those who do not live as though they follow Christ. At times our message comes across as judgmental. Too often we live independently from those around us who have genuine needs. For us to overcome these struggles, we should consider the example of the early church.

Luke, a doctor, historian, and adventurer within the early church, writes of the exploits of our Christian forefathers and foremothers:

> When the day of Pentecost came, they were all together in one place. Suddenly a sound like the blowing of a violent wind came from heaven and filled the whole house where they were sitting. They saw what seemed to be tongues of fire that separated and came to rest on each of them. All of them were filled with the Holy Spirit and began to speak in other tongues as the Spirit enabled them.
>
> Now there were staying in Jerusalem God-fearing Jews from every nation under heaven. When they heard this sound, a crowd came together in bewilderment, because each one heard their own language being spoken.
>
> **Acts 2:1 – 8**

These early followers of Christ were in relationships with others who did not know Christ. With the help of the miraculous, they shared with God-fearing Jews and converts who had come from all over the world to be part of a religious celebration called Pentecost. If we had been in their place, we probably would have enjoyed the wind and the gift of tongues for ourselves. Thinking, "Isn't this amazing what God is doing among us!" we may well have failed to venture out from being together in that "one place."

The early church didn't just talk about God's love; they actually loved people. Their reputation for generosity preceded them. People heard about the way these followers of the Way would sell their land and possessions and give the proceeds to meet the needs of others (see Acts 2:44 – 45). Their community included not only men, but women, slaves, and people from a variety of socioeconomic, political, and ethnic backgrounds as well. It should come as no surprise that the followers of Jesus would follow his example and soon after the miracle at Pentecost begin to go out to befriend and include religious zealots, pagans, tax collectors, Jews, Samaritans, Gentiles, Ethiopians, and so many others.

People who did not follow the Way respected those who did because of the way they loved each other and loved those who were not yet in their community.

As followers of Christ, we should be known by our love. As "the beloved disciple," John, grew older, he wrote letters to those close to him, preparing them to carry on without him. He writes, "Dear friends, let us love one another, for love comes from God. Everyone who loves has been born of God and knows God. Whoever does not love does not know God, because God is love" (1 John 4:7 – 8). God's character exudes love to such a degree that John writes that "God is love." In his very nature, God can be classified as "love."

Wouldn't it be amazing if people looked at our lives and described us in this way? To hear someone say, "She personifies love," or "If you looked up 'love' in the dictionary, you would see his picture."

When we are born into God's family, one of the most dominant genetic traits that becomes evident in our lives is love. If you want to discover whether you are related to God, just ask someone if they experience love from your life. Love is the greatest clue.

In the Scriptures, love isn't simply a warm feeling or even a choice of kindness. Love as defined and lived out by God involves sacrifice, as John illustrates:

> This is how God showed his love among us: He sent his one and only Son into the world that we might live through him. This is love: not that we loved God, but that he loved us and sent his Son as an atoning sacrifice for our sins. Dear friends, since God so loved us, we also ought to love one another. No one has ever seen God; but if we love one another, God lives in us and his love is made complete in us.
>
> 1 John 4:9 – 12

The apostle Paul also affirms this understanding of love when he writes, "But God demonstrates his own love for us in this: While we were still sinners, Christ died for us" (Romans 5:8).

Love equals sacrifice. We must be willing to lay down our lives for the sake of others (see John 15: 13). We must be willing to sacrifice our needs in order to meet the needs of others. The love others are to feel and experience around us is no less than love that actually costs us something. For too long, I have loved when it was convenient, expedient, or even strategic. To love to the point where it actually hurts connects more closely to what the word means. Love has been reduced to "like" or "lust." Genuine love requires genuine sacrifice.

The early church may have met in homes and hung out near the temple, but they also lived in the community and shared their lives with others who were not yet part of the Way. Too often we require others to come to us to find God rather than allowing what God does among us to spill over into the lives of those who have not been with us in that "one place."

Love is the new apologetic yet again. In a time when animosity toward followers of Christ seems to be rising, we need to live this out now more than ever. Some of the animosity we now experience may be, in reality, the displaced anger of those who have been hurt by others in the name of religion.

MATCHMAKING

Several years ago, a friend of mine named Erik Quillen asked me for advice. (We called him "EQ" in the office to avoid confusion between the two of us.) After he complained a bit about his lack of a love life, I decided to help him out. I wrote down the names of five women in our church and encouraged him to ask them out, one at a time. He could only complain again if his dating situation had not changed after he had finished asking out the women on this list. Most single guys I know complain, yet they never ask anyone out. I figured that giving them a list would keep them from coming back to me in the future. EQ was different — he actually did it!

He began by inviting the second woman on the list out on a date. Once that relationship seemed to be leading nowhere, he thought about his next move. After considering his previous experience with the third woman on the list and realizing he didn't even know who the fourth and fifth women were, he summoned the courage to invite the number one woman on his list, Holly, to dinner at the Cheesecake Factory. Deep inside, he had admired this person all along, but he had seen her as beyond his reach. Seventeen months later, EQ and Holly were married.

Since I am involved in a church where 80 percent of the attenders are single, you can imagine how many times someone asked me for a list. To dispel the myth of my prophetic nature as a cupid, I must finally reveal the secret of my list: I wrote down the names of the five women I suspected EQ already liked. I had seen him spending time with Holly in her office. Since they worked together, he would go in to get something, but he would come out twenty minutes later. Using my keen intellect, I put Holly at the top of his list.

I have to admit I like being a matchmaker, much to the dismay of my single friends, but when you have a good marriage, you want everyone to experience that amazing relationship. The same should be true in our relationship with Christ.

When someone has a great relationship with God, he or she should want others to enjoy and experience that relationship as well. We need to be willing to reallocate our time and energy because we are so in love with God that we want the people we care about to discover the same God we love and who loves us.

Paul was a matchmaker. As an apostle, Paul gave up his rights in order to freely serve and love others. Seeking to match up others with God, Paul wrote:

> Though I am free and belong to no one, I have made myself a slave to everyone, to win as many as possible. To the Jews I became like a Jew, to win the Jews. To those under the law I became like one under the law (though I myself am not under the law), so as to win those under the law. To those not having the law I became like one not having the law (though I am not free from God's law but am under Christ's law), so as to win those not having the law. To the weak I became weak, to win the weak. I have become all things to all people so that by all possible means I might save some.

> **1 Corinthians 9:19 – 22**

How different our lives would be if we went to such great lengths! We need to learn to share with others, naturally and in appropriate moments, how amazing a relationship with Jesus can be. We seem to openly refer others to movies or restaurants we enjoy, yet when it comes to spiritual conversations, we seem to slip into a "don't ask, don't tell" policy. Internally, we should be more motivated to become matchmakers.

There was once a broken and paralyzed man in Galilee who had some very caring friends. In a time when someone with a disability was considered cursed by God, these friends refused to walk away. They had heard that a man named Jesus was healing people. Helping their disabled friend get on a mat, they picked him up and walked a great distance to find this gentle Healer. A crowd surrounded the house in which Jesus stood. These friends decided not to give up. "We've come this far, so why stop now?" they must have concluded. Climbing onto the roof, they tore the roof apart to make a hole large enough to lower their friend in front of Jesus. This was the moment they had been waiting for. All the walking, carrying, roof digging, and sweating had been worth it. Jesus was going to heal their friend!

Jesus astonished the paralyzed man, his friends, and the entire crowd gathered in that home when he offered the paralyzed man forgiveness for his sins. Certainly the friends must have been filled with bitterness in that moment. Their friend needed new legs, not a new heart, yet Jesus reminded the crowd that the greatest miracle is a transformed life (see Luke 5:17 – 26).

Often we long to experience more of the miraculous — wanting to see people healed of their afflictions or even to be healed of our own. In doing so, we overlook or downplay the greatest miracle Christ offered as he walked the earth and the greatest miracle he offers to all of us today. What do all of those Jesus healed of leprosy, blindness, paralysis, and even death have in common now? They are all dead. But a heart transformed by God lives forever. God still physically heals people today. Physical healing doesn't last; spiritual healing does.

As the religious leaders' anger poured out in their venomous words against Jesus, Jesus decided to heal the paralyzed man physically too. Standing up, the man who was once paralyzed now walked home with his friends, the ones who were willing to carry him to meet Jesus.

If we want to become better matchmakers who passionately desire to help others discover the hope we have in Christ, we *must* learn to love. We must go to great lengths to serve and to meet the needs of friends — even to the point of being willing to pick them up and carry them if that's what it takes.

FIELD NOTES

A few years ago I woke up one Sunday and realized that, as much as I loved Jesus and enjoyed the volunteer work I was doing, nothing about my life existed outside of my church world. I couldn't name a friend who didn't have the same faith I did.

I had great friends, but I needed a few new ones. I was doing good things, but I longed to be stretched, challenged, pushed. I wanted answers, but more than anything I think I wanted questions. I stumbled onto the kind of blog that gets so much traffic that the speed of its replies felt more like a chat room. I lurked at first, reading the comments and devising my own responses to the smartly and sarcastically written blog posts. It took me weeks to find the courage to post anything on my own, but I was in, joining the conversation and, unbeknownst to me, the community.

I read BoredtoDeath's stories of his two failed marriages, laughed out loud at msdiva's joys and ills of single parenthood, and rolled my eyes at playa473 and his constant conquests that were simultaneously ego boosting and empty. I found myself sharing my own failed relationships and even being encouraged to forgive by a few posters who didn't profess to be Christians. For the first time in a long time, I had to articulate what it meant to have a relationship with God, using everyday language anybody could understand. These posters helped me become more honest, real, down-to-earth. More loving and accepting and way less judgmental. They had no idea, but they helped me become more like Jesus.

It's not a matter of God, them, and us; it's God and us — all of us living, breathing, mistake-making human beings. You don't come closer to knowing Jesus because of how close to perfect you are. Your first goal is to understand, listen, accept, and love. Then not only can you share the words of Jesus' message; you can demonstrate its reality by really loving people just as they are, and presenting yourself not as some know-it-all holier-than-thou but as a human being who needs God as much as anyone. It's funny how a website with pseudonyms helped me become more real than I had been in a long time. Maybe people who don't believe in Jesus but are searching for something real in their lives want someone to love and keep it real with them. Maybe this is what Jesus wants too.

Amena Brown

As a performance poet, speaker, and arts journalist, Amena Brown lends her voice to finding inspiration, truth, and purpose as she encourages those she encounters to do the same. Visit Amena at *www.amenabrown.com; www.myspace.com/amenabrown.*

Chapter 2

BOUNCE HOUSES IN THE NEIGHBORHOOD

Getting off the Couch to Make Friends

When our family first moved into our home in Alhambra, a city in the middle of Los Angeles County, I was excited to meet our new neighbors. As we unpacked our boxes, I fully expected at any minute they would knock at our front door with cookies or cupcakes, or any sort of treat, as a housewarming gift. Day after day, the number of boxes to unpack diminished, yet we heard no knock at the door. After a couple of weeks, we were completely moved in and had yet to meet our neighbors. I was saddened and surprised. Perhaps I was also naive.

My theory is that since the invention of the garage door opener, neighbors across the country have slowly slipped out of each other's lives. As men and women open their garage door with the push of a button from the front seat of their car, they can easily disappear into their homes without ever having to walk up their driveway and see another neighbor on the same trek. People can live close to other people yet never truly know them. They might know their names, but they don't know what brings them joy or sadness.

My neighborhood has since disproved my theory — there are no garage door openers on our street! The houses and garages were built in the 1920s before cars became sport utility vehicles. As a result, almost everyone parks their cars in their driveway or along the street. Yet we still had not even introduced ourselves to those living around us. Garage door openers hadn't ruined neighborliness; neighbors had.

Voicing my disappointment to my wife, Debbie, she came up with a brilliant idea: *we* would bake cookies and take them to our neighbors. Instead of feeling sorry for ourselves, we would start acting the way we had expected our neighbors to act. Isn't there a passage in the Bible where Jesus challenges us to do to others as we would have them do to us? Debbie's idea was to actually try this out. Why hadn't I thought of that? I agreed under one condition: we must bake at least one batch for ourselves. We were the ones who were new to the neighborhood, and I felt we deserved some cookies.

The next day, we set off to meet our neighbors. As odd as we may have looked as we ventured out as strangers with gifts of homemade cookies, I have to admit we were hard to resist. Our son, Caleb, was two years old and starting to say some of the cutest little words. He had beautiful curly hair since he had yet to have his first haircut. What's more, Debbie was just starting to waddle as a result of her pregnant belly. With Debbie and Caleb standing in front of me, we knocked on the doors of about six homes. Every single person was exceedingly warm and grateful and welcoming to us. I wished we had done this sooner!

A few weeks later, Sonny, one of our new neighbors, revealed to me a reason for the lack of hospitality: he had been scared of us. I was confused. How could anyone be intimidated by our family? It turned out that Sonny thought we were the same people who had lived there before. Not seeing us move in, he didn't realize we were new to the neighborhood. The previous owners were white, like we are. Since there are only about ten white people in the entire five square blocks, he just assumed we were the same people. Sonny went on to explain that the couple who lived in our house before us never seemed happy with the neighborhood. In fact, they had received special permission from the city to build a large wooden fence around the backyard, an unusual request in a neighborhood with only chain-link fences. Plus, they always seemed to hurry in and out of their house. As a result, he was intimidated by them. Once we brought over cookies, he realized we were quite friendly and were, in fact, a different family.

The cookies we took to our neighbors that day represented a tremendous breakthrough, but it was just the beginning. I would purposely mow the lawn, water the grass, and play with the kids in the front yard during the times that others would be outside or coming home from work so we could interact with them. Now as we drive through the neighborhood, my wife, who is introverted, comments that she feels as though she is in a parade, having to wave to all who pass by.

THE NEIGHBORHOOD GANG

A few years ago, Debbie and I celebrated our anniversary by traveling to Hawaii, one of the few places in the world that actually lives up to the hype. Upon our return, we expected to hear great stories of time spent between grandparents and their grandkids. For the most part, my parents had enjoyed a great experience babysitting. They always graciously agreed to spend time with our kids, who were four and one at the time. (You really have to be related to someone to care for kids at that age for an extended period of time!)

In addition to their adventures at the zoo, at the park, on the merry-go-round, and on the train rides, my mom was eager to share with us something horrible that had happened: *Caleb was attacked with sticks by a gang.* He wasn't injured, but apparently it was a close call.

Debbie and I looked at each other, perplexed and confused. A gang had attacked Caleb? Our street has always been remarkably safe and calm, at least in terms of Los Angeles County standards. There has been an occasional carjacking, graffiti tagged in a few spots, a couple of homeless people here and there, a few drug busts, and only two homicides; but all in all, our neighborhood is a great place to live. Since getting to know our neighbors better, we discovered that they are just like us — with jobs and kids. They enjoy a good dinner with friends; reality shows, sitcoms, and dramas on TV; a good movie on the weekend; an occasional trip to the beaches in the summer; and the Dodgers and Clippers (well, some like the Angels, and actually most like the Lakers). Several of our neighbors have lived in their homes for thirty-plus years, including several who purchased their homes from their parents. We have a good neighborhood; no, I would say we live in a great neighborhood. This made the story of the gang attack seem so out of place.

Trying to get to the bottom of the attack that my mom alerted us to, we walked to the end of the street with Caleb. It was then that I saw the "gang." Standing on the lawn of their apartment building, wearing only shorts and holding sticks, I saw four little Asian boys.

In that moment, I understood my mom's concerns. Even though these guys were quite small, I still felt a strong desire to protect my son.Before I could stop him, Caleb ran over to them. We hadn't met these little guys before, but apparently, like Caleb, they were big Star Wars fans. The sticks they were swinging toward Caleb were light sabers. I could tell Caleb was about to claim that he was Darth Vader. Caleb's love for the dark lord makes me nervous. I keep reminding Caleb, myself, and anyone who looks at him curiously that in the end Darth Vader became a good guy. Regardless, on that day with those kids in our neighborhood, the Force was with us: it appeared Caleb was welcome to join "the gang."

My mom and I, like all of us do, jumped to conclusions as a result of being in an unfamiliar environment. Seeing those little guys swinging sticks at Caleb created a moment of anxiety for both of us. In that context, how could we have known that these boys wanted to play rather than to attack? Too often, we let our assumptions come between us and others. In doing so, we miss great relationships with others. Perhaps we should follow the lead of our children. They seem to assume the best and not even hesitate to become friends with other kids in the neighborhood.

WON'T YOU BE MY NEIGHBOR?

Apparently, Mr. Rogers, the maven of neighborliness for my generation, knew Jesus. The man who played Mr. Rogers for all those years had studied to become a Presbyterian minister; his full name was Frederick McFeely Rogers. Rather than participating in a ministry in which he spoke to adults at a church, he taught children via the television set. Honestly, I always felt that Mr. Rogers seemed sort of dull, but many others really enjoyed him. Regardless of what you thought of him, for anyone who ever watched this middle-aged man who slipped into a cardigan and changed into tennis shoes, Mr. Rogers reminded us of what was important: Being someone's neighbor meant becoming someone's friend.

In the New Testament, when asked to give a CliffsNotes version of the Hebrew Scriptures, Jesus threw a bit of a curveball. An expert in the law asked Jesus, "Of all the commandments, which is the most important?" (Mark 12:28). Jesus responded with not one but two commandments, or perhaps two different sides to the same coin: "Love the Lord your God .... Love your neighbor." To Jesus' way of thinking, people cannot love God and hate their neighbors. On the flip side, to love our neighbors fully, we must connect to God. Our relationships with God and other people are intimately connected and not mutually exclusive. We need God *and* people.

As Jesus walked the earth, he didn't merely spend his time with the Father; he recruited others to follow him, to spend life with him. He then mobilized these friends to go out with him to the crowds and to the cities where people needed love and attention.

Sadly, rather than follow Christ's example, too often we tend to move in the opposite direction. We move *away* from the crowds and into a cluster of friends who believe and live just like we do. Then, when these friends hurt us, as is inevitable in human relationships, some of us retreat into our homes. We rationalize that all we need is just God himself. We conclude that we don't need to be part of a church, and we certainly don't need to reach out. We justify to ourselves that to be truly spiritual, we must simply commune with God by ourselves.

In reality, the more we truly connect with God's heart, the more he will send us out into relationships with other followers of Christ and with those who do not yet follow Christ. When we run to God, he sends us out. As we experience rejection or hardship, we run to God so that, after refreshing us and bandaging our wounds, he can send us out again, perhaps stronger and wiser.

Continuing to astonish his listeners, Jesus defines "neighbor" in another conversation by telling the parable of the good Samaritan (see Luke 10:25 – 37). A man attacked by robbers was left bleeding on the side of the road. A priest and a Levite — religious leaders — passed by without offering any assistance, but a Samaritan — an enemy — offered mercy to the beaten man. In this context, a neighbor is someone who breaks through social barriers to meet the needs of another person. In essence, Jesus tells us to love our neighbor — and that we have more neighbors than we realize.

Since we live in a rapidly changing and diversifying world, getting off the couch poses new challenges. Though there still may be many shared similarities, when your neighbors are from different cultures, it requires a willingness to step into uncertainty and make sacrifices.

Getting to know my own neighbors beyond waving "hello" from afar has created amazing opportunities, such as eating chicken feet and dim sum (Chinese appetizers), bamboo shoots and tripe, and some sort of noodle dish with pork joints at Noodle Planet, just to name a few. By stepping into another person's culture, we are stepping into their world and into their lives. Too often we act as though the way our mom cooks is the only acceptable method. Our ethnocentricity keeps us from engaging in new experiences and, more important, new relationships.

The apostle Peter knew something about taking risks and experiencing new food, though not without first having to overcome his own ethnocentric tendencies. Paul shares a story in his letter to the Galatians about a time when he confronted Peter publicly. Peter chose to hide his relationships with Gentiles when some of the

Judaizers came to visit him. The Judaizers wanted to mandate that all Gentiles who wished to follow Jesus must first become Jewish (i.e., become circumcised; see Acts 15:1). Can you imagine if they would have won the argument and the early church had sided with them? Ouch!

In a moment of weakness, Peter decided to avoid standing up on behalf of his Gentile friends and instead acted as though he didn't know them (sounds similar to the time when he denied that he knew Jesus after Jesus was arrested; see John 18). Paul's confrontation with Peter reminds us of the importance of embracing others — even those with whom we differ or disagree or whom we don't know, and even when doing so creates discomfort for ourselves (see Galatians 2:11 – 21).

Peter may not have even ventured to befriend Gentiles at all had he not experienced a miraculous moment from God that mobilized him to meet a new neighbor. Cornelius, an Italian soldier, saw a vision that sent him on a mission to find Peter. Cornelius eagerly pursued God through prayer and acts of kindness toward the poor, but he had a huge problem: Cornelius was a Gentile, and Peter saw Gentiles as unclean.

Knowing that Peter was apt to give Cornelius's servants a less than neighborly welcome once they arrived, God gave Peter a vision as well. Proving the saying that "a way to a man's heart is through his stomach," God filled Peter's mind with thoughts of delicious yet unclean foods. As his stomach growled with hunger, Peter saw a large feast coming down from heaven. Three times Peter saw this heavenly banquet, yet he refused to enjoy anything "unclean" — only to be encouraged to "go ahead and eat." For some reason, Peter and most of us as well need to be told things at least three times before we get it. In the end, Peter understood the intention of the trance: "Do not call anything impure that God has made clean"

(Acts 10:15). God wasn't just hoping Peter would begin enjoying a wider variety of foods; God wanted Peter to embrace the people who already enjoyed those foods. God wanted Peter to step out of his comfort zone and get involved in the lives of people he had previously overlooked.

Peter not only invited Cornelius's servants into his house; he went into Cornelius's house the next day as well. Peter willingly stepped into the house of someone considered unworthy, knowing he would later be criticized and judged by other believers (see Acts 11:2). In front of the crowd assembled at Cornelius's house, Peter declared, "I now realize how true it is that God does not show favoritism but accepts those from every nation who fear him and do what is right" (Acts 10:34). That day, Cornelius's friends and relatives — all who heard Peter's message — were transformed by God. They received a miraculous moment from the Holy Spirit and were baptized. Furthermore, Peter would never be the same.

God moved in mystical and marvelous ways to connect Peter and Cornelius, yet Peter still had to act. He chose to welcome Gentiles and to be welcomed into the houses of Gentiles. Later, once the leaders of the early church moved closer to making a decision about the Gentiles, Peter became a major proponent of salvation by grace rather than requiring circumcision as a prerequisite for salvation (see Acts 15:1). As a result, the church and the world would never be the same.

THE SPIDERMAN BOUNCE HOUSE

Rather than a vision from God motivating me to leave my house to interact with and minister to a neighbor, as Peter experienced, God used my little boy, who loved Spiderman bounce houses.

Bounce houses and piñatas must be mandatory for all birthday parties in Los Angeles. There are several kids in our neighborhood who are the same age as our kids, so we have had many birthday parties on our block, and they almost always include bounce houses and piñatas. We discovered this firsthand when we crashed one of our neighbors' parties.

Caleb was still learning to speak that first summer in our neighborhood, but one phrase he knew was "bounce house." It didn't sound quite like that when he said it, but I knew what he meant as he started pointing and screaming at the one he saw down the street. We had never met this family, but Caleb would not stop screaming and crying and demanding a chance to jump in the bounce house. To make matters worse, it was a Spiderman bounce house.

I will never understand why children who can hardly speak and have never even seen Tobey Maguire in action love Spiderman so much. Zane, one of our friends' kids, changed the lyrics of a popular song from "Lord God Almighty" to "Lord God All Spidey." This was no cute slip of the tongue but intentional. Another friend of ours has a little guy named Jakob. When asked if he wanted to ask Jesus into his heart as a three-year-old boy, he responded, "No, I want to ask Spiderman into my heart." Like his buddies Zane and Jakob, Caleb worshiped Spiderman. Add to that the possibility of jumping around inside a giant Spiderman bounce house, and Caleb must have felt that he had reached his paradise.

Realizing it would be easier to approach a complete stranger to see if Caleb could jump than it would be to get him to stop screaming, I walked my little persuasive and pagan guy down the street. Since no one was outside, I considered just sneaking Caleb into the bounce house without asking. If I got caught, I would just point and blame Caleb for our intrusive and rude behavior. I realized that this was a bad idea and knocked on the door to see if we could crash their party, at least long enough for Caleb to jump around for a few minutes.

Busily preparing for their son Sebastian's party, our neighbors Isai and Valerie Guzman not only graciously allowed Caleb to get inside the bounce house but also insisted that we stay for the party. My plan had been to just let him jump for five or maybe even ten minutes before sneaking away.

As Caleb jumped, I checked with the Guzmans to see if I could help them in any way. They seemed to have everything under control, so I ventured back outside to check on Caleb. He was insisting I join him, so I took off my shoes and crawled in. Entering the web between Spiderman's arms, I was stunned. The entire floor of the bounce house was covered in milk. Caleb's gastrostomy tube (also known as a G-tube) had come unplugged.

As an infant, Caleb had to have open-heart surgery. After spending the first two months of his life in the hospital, he was finally able to come home with us. Unfortunately, he had not been able to nurse or even drink milk from a bottle during those first couple of months, because his heart and lungs had been working so hard just to keep him alive. As a result, Caleb had to learn certain things that are normally instinctive for babies. For the next three and a half years, Caleb took his nourishment through a feeding tube connected to his stomach while he learned to eat and drink by mouth.

Feeding Caleb through a feeding tube and teaching him how to eat with the help of many amazing doctors and occupational therapists posed quite a challenge, but it also had some advantages. When Caleb was an infant, we would connect the machine filled with milk to his feeding tube. While most parents are awakened at all hours of the night by screaming babies who want to be fed, our little Caleb would sleep for ten to twelve hours every night as the milk dripped into his tummy.

On this particular day, however, the G-tube was absolutely not advantageous. All of the milk inside of his little stomach had just flowed out of his tiny tube onto the bouncy floor. Not only was Caleb bouncing in this undigested milk; soon other kids would be arriving to take their turns. We were about to ruin Sebastian's first birthday.

I was wearing two shirts, so I quickly took off the top one to mop up the mess. It was amazing how much milk his little stomach could hold! Just before I got my undershirt off as well, Isai walked outside. Realizing I was going to have to explain what had happened, I apologized profusely and shared with him about Caleb's medical problems. I was hoping he might not get too upset if I could get him to feel sorry for us. My plea for sympathy was unnecessary. Rather than expressing rage or disgust, he hurried inside to grab some paper towels.

As I finished the job of cleaning up the slippery, milky mess, Isai and I discovered something we had in common that was quite fascinating. Isai's older son, Isaiah, and Caleb were both born on the same day in the same year, and both actually spent time in the same neonatal intensive care unit at the same time! In spite of our unusual introduction, we became fast friends.

SUBURBAN, URBAN, OR RURAL

Since according to Jesus, our neighbors do not just include those who live near us, we need to be more intentional about broadening the scope of our neighborhood. At the same time, we can start by serving those who live next to us. Where we live provides natural opportunities to engage with others.

Over the past few years, I seem to be meeting more and more people who choose their neighborhood as a place for ministry rather than simply as a place to have a house and catch some sleep at night. On the other end of the spectrum, too often I meet Christians who are just like everyone else, choosing to live in the places that provide the greatest safety and convenience or have the highest rated school districts. Then, as we have more income, we move out of our current locations so we can have even greater safety and convenience and even better school districts. This very natural way of living, sadly, has a way of circumventing the impact we can have in our neighborhoods. We end up looking at our neighborhoods for what we get rather than seeing them as places where we can find opportunities to give and to serve. We should think more like John F. Kennedy thought: "Ask not what your neighborhood can do for you, but what you can do for your neighborhood."

For evangelical Christians, this "search for safety" temptation can be particularly enticing. In fact, evangelicals created the suburb. Perhaps this should have been obvious, since over the past several decades, churches have been moving out of the inner cities and into the suburbs. As some of the same elements we have tried to avoid (crime, gangs, graffiti, bad schools, etc.) have followed us, we have moved even farther away. Our suburbs are now blending into what used to be rural areas.

This pattern can be seen already in the late eighteenth century outside of London, England. Evangelical Christian leaders called for the creation of towns isolated from "the dangers, cruelties, bad language, suffering, and immorality that filled the crowded London streets."[1] They sought to create a place "dedicated to the ideals of domestic purity."[2]

In their zeal for God, these eighteenth-century evangelicals separated themselves from the world. They applied 1 John 2:15 – 16 to their living situation: "Do not love the world or anything in the world. If you love the world, love for the Father is not in you. For everything in the world — the cravings of sinful people, the lust of their eyes and their boasting of what they have and do — comes not from the Father but from the world." Instead, we should apply this verse to how we live our lives, not to where we live. Our character and actions should be what sets us apart — not our zip code.

In our attempts to become holy or "set apart," we have mistaken a call for "living with a different standard" with "living in a different place that has a different standard." We want to live in an environment where the laws or policies enforce our beliefs and morality rather than engaging a lost and broken world where they live. And if we are to be "set apart" to be "apostles," in the broad sense of people who are "sent out," then we are to be "set apart" in how we live, and we are "sent out" to the world. Too often we reverse these two concepts. We live away from the world physically, but our behavior matches that of the world.

The same apostle John who has several letters preserved in the Bible wrote in his gospel about God's love for the world and Jesus' role as light in the world:

> The true light [Jesus] that gives light to everyone was coming into the world.
>
> **John 1:9**

> For God so loved the world that he gave his one and only Son [Jesus], that whoever believes in him shall not perish but have eternal life.
>
> **John 3:16**

While I [Jesus] am in the world, I am the light of the world.

John 9:5

Jesus reminds us that we have the same purpose he had — to be a light in this world:

You are the light of the world. A city on a hill cannot be hidden. Neither do people light a lamp and put it under a bowl. Instead they put it on its stand, and it gives light to everyone in the house. In the same way, let your light shine before others, that they may see your good deeds and glorify your Father in heaven.

Matthew 5:14 – 16

If a light cannot be seen under a bowl, it's certainly not visible hiding in a commune, in a church building, or on the other side of the freeway.

If we look back at the early church, we discover that the movement of the good news about Christ spread as the church moved into new neighborhoods and new communities. After a great persecution, followers of the Way scattered to new locations: "Those who had been scattered preached the word wherever they went" (Acts 8:4).

Rather than creating communities that exclude those who do not believe the same things we believe or act the same way we act, we should infiltrate communities to become light in that part of the world. Whether we intentionally move into an impoverished area or intentionally move into a gated community in a wealthy part of town — or anywhere in between — wherever we go, that is our mission field.

There are too many inner-city, suburban, and rural churches acting as places of refuge from the world. We need more churches that see themselves as lights in their communities, no matter where they might be.

We need to create genuine relationships with those near us, and we need to be near those who need us. We need people moving into the high-rent districts, not to avoid the rest of us but to reach those who are there; we need people moving into impoverished areas to show God's love. Both will require different types of sacrifices. We need people to rise up where they are to serve, to love, and to be a neighbor in the way Jesus intends us to be.

NEIGHBORS = FRIENDS

The simple idea of building friendships may seem odd, but our world is filled with broken relationships and loneliness. Perhaps we should stop and consider how well we even know those we call our friends. Many of us fall into a trap of superficiality.

Even in cities with millions of people milling around, men and women go through their day without one meaningful interaction or even a single experience of human touch. Perhaps this is especially true in cities with millions of people. We all assume that the people around us must have others in their lives, when in reality, the feeling of loneliness grows like a fog over their hearts.

Several years ago, a middle-aged man was riding in a crowded subway train in New York City when he instantly died from a heart attack. His body slumped over, leaning next to the window. For the next six hours, his lifeless body rode along without anyone noticing. It wasn't until the subway driver pulled into the station at the end of his shift that paramedics were called to help this man who had stopped breathing. Obviously, it was way too late.

While reading a book about Los Angeles after moving here in

1998, I was not surprised to learn that many people in Los Angeles live in isolation. The book mentioned that people can live in the same place for ten years and never even know their neighbor's name. What did surprise me was the date the book was published — 1930.

The histories of our city and innumerable cities around the world include stories of millions of people who are lonely and depressed, alone even though they are surrounded by lots of other people. Perhaps because there are so many people, we assume that everyone we see must have a friend, even though many do not. We live in the midst of a crowd of loners.

In our day, the term "neighbor" no longer has a warm connotation implying someone near you who is trustworthy or friendly. Across our country, we have redefined what it means to be a neighbor. The way we often live our isolated lives has shifted the meaning of "neighbor" to simply refer to the people who live in close proximity. We need to recapture and redefine the word "neighbor "to include friendship.

Over the past several years, we have grown to love our neighbors. Some of our best friends are, in fact, our neighbors. We go out to dinner with them, have each other over, watch *Lost* together, babysit for each other, enjoy movies at the theater together, and celebrate birthdays and even Christmas Eves together. One of the families in our neighborhood now goes to church with us, and their daughter Isabella was baptized last year. Our kids play T-ball together, and we play softball together.

Actually, the softball team from our neighborhood won our church's softball tournament two years in a row. In our attempt to three-peat, we lost as a result of some controversial calls (although I promise I will one day overcome my bitterness). After inviting some of the guys to play with us for the first time, I realized I should have told them the tournament was sponsored by my church. After using their normal colorful language while describing our strategy, they seemed shocked and embarrassed when the leader of the event referred to me as "one of the pastors" and asked me to pray.

In spite of occasional hiccups like this, we have found genuine friendship among our neighbors, and as a result, we have been able to have natural conversations about every aspect of life. Through these relationships, we have seen lives changed — especially our own. Life is much more fun across the street than on our couch.

FIELD NOTES

Every city street and rural road has its own story to tell. This chapter is overflowing with practical life messages that pour out of a powerful neighborhood narrative. Eric has captured the voice of his community and drawn out lessons that will transfer naturally to where you live.

As I read this chapter, I heard God speak and call me to love my community with greater passion. Here are some of the messages I heard:

Don't wait for people to reach out to you. Take the first step, and see what happens. I love the fact that Eric and Debbie made cookies and knocked on their neighbors' doors. Conventional wisdom says that people don't want to be bothered. Sometimes conventional wisdom is wrong. I suspect that many of our neighbors would love it if someone reached out to them in a practical and tangible way (and cookies never hurt the process).

Action Idea. Soon, my wife and I will begin ministry in a new place and will move into a new neighborhood. We are not going to wait for the greeting committee to come over (because we will be waiting a long time), but we will take the initiative and bring a small gift to the people who live in the homes right near us. We will pray and go, trusting that God will go before us and build a relational bridge. If you have a neighbor you don't know, take a chance, reach out, and see what happens.

Natural family connections are infinitely valuable. Let your kids connect naturally in your community and follow their lead — even if it means seeing them join a gang of Jedis! When my boys were young, they all played soccer in the community AYSO league. I coached more than twenty teams in the span of a decade. God forged hundreds of connections and friendships in our community through our boys' participation on these teams and my role as a coach.

Action Idea. If you have children who are involved in your community through sports, the arts, clubs, or some other activity, pray for this to become a way for you to build relationships with families and parents. Make time. Linger after events. Talk with the other parents. If your kids are only in church (or church school) activities, consider being intentional about signing them up for something in the community. As you do, pray for the people you meet and make time to get to know them. You will be amazed at the doors God opens through these contacts.

Explore new cultures, styles, and traditions. Let the door swing both ways. Be sure to invite people into your home, life, and even your church. But don't be shy about entering their homes and walking with them on their journeys. We need to be like our Savior, who loved to enter people's lives, explore their landscapes, break bread in their homes, and experience their cultures.

Action Idea. Say yes when people invite you into their lives. Go to their homes, enter their worlds, and even explore their cultural landscapes. Try something new and take risks for Jesus. Our Savior was accused of being a glutton and a drunkard and was called a friend of sinners (Luke 7:34). Wouldn't it be wonderful if we were so immersed in our communities and the lives of our neighbors that people made similar accusations about us?

God's people are needed in neighborhoods of every type. Faithful and Christ-honoring people can be called to live in every imaginable location. The big issue is not the actual place, but believers bringing God's presence wherever he places us. God will send his people to the cities, rural farming communities, suburbs, gated neighborhoods, executive high-rises, apartment complexes, trailer parks, and everywhere people need to encounter the person and message of Jesus. Our job is not to criticize where God sends someone else but to fully engage where God has placed us.

Action Idea. See your neighborhood as a mission field. Short-term mission trips have become popular (and this is fine). But wouldn't it be amazing if all Christians saw the places where they live as mission fields? When we have this outlook, every day becomes an adventure and every new encounter a time for the Spirit of God to show up and do something fresh and new. When we get off the couch and cross the street, we might just be on a mission trip!

Kevin Harney

Kevin is lead pastor of Shoreline Community Church in Monterey, California. He is the author of *Organic Outreach*, *Seismic Shifts*, and more than sixty small group studies and curriculum resources. Find Kevin at *www.OrganicOutreach.org*.

Chapter 3

PEPPERMINT-FILLED PIÑATAS

Partying to Expand Our Influence

I'm an outgoing guy, so you would think I'd have a knack for throwing generous parties. But generally, when you host a party, you have to feed your guests. Parties cost money. Giving in to my tightwad tendencies, last year I tried to figure out how to combine multiple holidays into one big party. There was Mother's Day, Father's Day, my daughter's birthday in June, the Fourth of July, my son's birthday in July, plus Memorial Day and Labor Day at the beginning and end of summer. Putting them into one sort of Summer Fest would save me a great deal of money, not to mention the time spent standing next to the grill. I tried to explain to Debbie that several of these holidays were manufactured by Hallmark and the federal government to increase consumer spending during the lagging summer months, but she refused to support my idea. In the end, I was able only to combine the kids' birthday parties.

During the preparations, Debbie sent me out to get candy for the piñata. (She didn't trust me with much else.) My kids love piñatas. At one recent party with a Tinkerbell piñata, our daughter, Trevi, the smallest and therefore first child in line, timidly and sweetly picked up the stick and turned into a samurai warrior. With both hands wrapped around the pole, her face focused and contorted, she jumped off the ground, hitting Tinkerbell's neck before the helpers even had a chance to raise the four-foot-tall piñata off the ground. My son (who had years earlier cried when we forced him to bludgeon Blue from the children's TV show *Blue's Clues*) shouted encouragement: "Knock her head off!"

When I had gone out shopping for the party, I figured that the act of breaking the piñata interested kids more than the actual prizes found inside. So I looked for a good deal. Much to my excitement, I found three bags containing a total of six hundred peppermints for only $6. "These kids just want something sweet," I reasoned.

As soon as I came home, Debbie immediately stopped what she was doing and raced over to the store to buy "real candy." My wife never swears, but she seemed to consider yielding to the temptation in that moment.

A PARTY THEOLOGY

I learned a valuable lesson that day. Peppermints do not belong in piñatas. Still trying to get rid of hundreds of peppermints four months later, I discovered that kids don't really want them in their Halloween bags either. I thought kids cared more about smashing the piñata than about the contents of the piñata. I guess I had over-looked the dozens of times I had to hold back the kids in line who raced toward the candy falling out of the piñata, even as the blind-folded kid kept swinging the bat wildly. These kids couldn't care less about the danger; they wanted the prizes! They loved hitting the piñata and eating the yummy candy strewn across the yard.

Too often in the church, we fall into the same trap I did. We ask others to exert a tremendous amount of effort, even though the results of these efforts remain less than desirable. We think others are willing to connect with us, even though what we offer is cheap and unsat-isfying. We offer peppermints, when the world wants Gobstoppers, Airheads, and Reese's Peanut Butter Cups. We offer something sweet to believe; they want a new life that helps change the world.

The world too often sees the invitation to connect to the church as irrelevant or at best as involving a cumbersome process. People have to learn our religious language, sing our songs, and discuss our topics. For those who make the effort to connect with us, we reward them with rules, traditions, and conditional acceptance, yet Jesus offered grace, forgiveness, and love. Rather than religion, Jesus offers relationship. As part of the body called the church, we need to strive to eliminate barriers that keep others from connecting with our community and connecting with Jesus.

In the end, no thanks to me, we hosted a great party, and I dis-covered that saving money is not as important as creating a fun place where my kids and our friends and neighbors can interact. By offer-ing a peppermint-filled piñata, I was doing as little as possible to simply "get by" rather than spending the time and money needed to create an experience the kids would enjoy. I was willing to do just enough to meet minimal expectations. Thankfully, Debbie saved the moment with her generosity.

We can eliminate barriers and develop life-transforming relationships as we emphasize the importance of relationships by throwing more parties that follow Levi's example:[1]

> After this, Jesus went out and saw a tax collector by the name of Levi sitting at his tax booth. "Follow me," Jesus said to him, and Levi got up, left everything and followed him.
>
> Then Levi held a great banquet for Jesus at his house, and a large crowd of tax collectors and others were eating with them. But the Pharisees and the teachers of the law who belonged to their sect complained to his disciples, "Why do you eat and drink with tax collectors and sinners?"
>
> Jesus answered them, "It is not the healthy who need a doctor, but the sick. I have not come to call the righteous, but sinners to repentance."
>
> **Luke 5:27 – 32**

After spending time healing people and teaching with insight, serving both the religious leaders and those who were broken, Jesus encountered a reviled tax collector. Perhaps as a result of Jesus' reputation or an intrinsic desire for something more, Levi (who was also known as Matthew) immediately responded to Jesus' invitation and got up to follow him. Levi's new relationship with Jesus created a desire to help his friends discover what he had discovered, so he threw a party for Jesus and invited the only friends a tax collector would have in those days — other tax collectors and sinners. He wanted them to meet the same Jesus who had changed his life.

Like Levi, we should throw parties for Jesus — parties *on behalf of* Jesus — by inviting those who are disconnected and lonely and who need a friend. We must create opportunities to serve and to love, and to introduce people to the living God through our relationships.

God is found through people. God's Spirit resides within those who follow him. Of course, God makes himself known in many different ways, through his creation, signs, visions, and the deep longings we feel inside, yet at the same time, he has created us as interactive and interconnected beings. God chooses to spread his message of love and hope through the lives of those who have experienced him. We meet God and introduce him to others in the context of our friendships.

OIKOS

Our parties should include our *oikos* — our families, friends, neighbors, and coworkers. In the New Testament, the Greek word *oikos* is often translated "house" or "household." In our Western mind-set, we consider a "household" as simply parents and their children, yet a more accurate understanding would be one's entire sphere of influence. When someone chose to follow Christ, the person was rarely alone — the royal official, Cornelius, the Italian soldier, Lydia, and the synagogue ruler Crispus (see John 4:53; Acts 11:14; 16:15; 18:8) are just a few examples of people whose transformed lives led to the transformation of those they already knew, those within their "household."

I used to think that sharing my faith involved telling someone I had never met before about Jesus. We have all heard inspiring stories about people who lead the person seated next to them to follow Christ just as the airplane pulls into the gate. We often equate the experience Philip had with the Ethiopian eunuch (see Acts 8:26 – 39) with modern-day evangelism. But this is the exception rather than the rule.

Levi reveals an even more effective and more challenging method: serving, loving, and sharing Christ with those we already know. It's relatively easy to share your faith with someone you will never see again, but it is extremely difficult to share with someone you will see again the next day. And it is even more difficult to share with someone who knows how we actually live our lives. An uncomfortable level of accountability comes once we share about our relationship with Jesus with someone we know.

Levi invited other tax collectors to his party because that was the world he knew. His party reminds us to become even more intentional and engaged with those we already know.

BEYOND *OIKOS* TO *XENOS*

Always being challenged toward greater generosity, we discover that Jesus not only wants us to become generous with those we know; he wants us to become generous with those we don't know.

Jesus, the consummate party planner, tells more about his type of parties in the gospel of Luke:

> Then Jesus said to his host, "When you give a luncheon or dinner, do not invite your friends, your brothers or sisters, your relatives, or your rich neighbors; if you do, they may invite you back and so you will be repaid. But when you give a banquet, invite the poor, the crippled, the lame, the blind, and you will be blessed. Although they cannot repay you, you will be repaid at the resurrection of the righteous."
>
> **Luke 14:12 – 14**

A party theology includes a host who not only gives generously to the guests but has a generous invitation list. We need to go out and seek the people who need a friend and those who want or even need a party. Inviting friends and family makes sense, but we must not overlook the ones who are *xenos* (out there) who need to be *oikos* (in here) — the ones no one else has invited. *Xenos* is the Greek word for "stranger," "foreigner," or "alien." Discovering God's heart for the stranger shows us that we must also love those outside of our *oikos* and embrace the *xenos*.

One of the most unique *xenos*-turned-*oikos* relationships I've observed involved Jason. After watching *ER* at our friends' house (back when George Clooney was still operating on the small screen), I stopped to fill up our car with gas about 11:30 p.m. on the way home. Since this predated the "pay at the pump" option (and, of course, the outrageous gas prices), I walked inside to pay the thin white guy with multiple earrings and scraggly hair — Jason by name — who was working the night shift. Making superficial conversation, I asked him how he passed the time working the night shift. He responded with, "I've been reading through the Bible."

Caught a bit off guard, I asked where he had been reading. "I started in Genesis, and now I'm reading in First Cronthans." (Mispronouncing the word "Corinthians" should have been my clue that he was new to the Scriptures.) Intrigued and impressed that he had read so much, I asked him what he thought of his reading so far. He answered, "Well, there sure are a lot of [expletive] Israelite names."

Once again, I was a bit stunned, and now I was almost positive all this was new to him. I asked him where he had gotten his Bible, hoping a friend of his was helping him understand what he was reading, as well as helping him know more about a relationship with Jesus. "I stole it from my friend's dad." His answer finally confirmed my suspicions: he had not been in the habit of reading the Bible.

After introducing myself, I invited him to continue our conversation later in the week when he was off duty. I promised him that I would bring him a Bible, one that was easier to read, since he had been working his way through the King James Version. As we sat together a week or so later, I asked Jason if he believed in God. I will never forget his answer: "I never did, but now I know he is real because he is speaking to me through the Bible."

Jason, a stranger who worked at a gas station, soon became my friend. We talked a lot over the next several months. He was living with his girlfriend, who was pregnant with his child. His wife, with whom he had a daughter, was now living with another guy, and she was pregnant with the other guy's baby. Honestly, I didn't know how to help him. Should he divorce his wife to marry his girlfriend, or should he make things right with his wife? In the end, neither woman wanted him. They weren't interested in this new Jason.

Whenever I think of meeting Jason as a stranger and then seeing the transformation in his life, I cannot help but think of the verse that says, "Do not forget to show hospitality to strangers, for by so doing some people have shown hospitality to angels without knowing it" (Hebrews 13:2). Granted, he would have been a fallen angel, but even so, meeting him and being allowed to play a small part in his life remain one of the most mystical and special experiences of my life.

Throughout the Scriptures, we discover God's heart for the stranger, the outcast, the foreigner. When choosing to bless Abram, God promised, "I will make you into a great nation and I will bless you; I will make your name great, and you will be a blessing. I will bless those who bless you, and whoever curses you I will curse; and *all peoples on earth* will be blessed through you" (Genesis 12:2–3, emphasis mine). God did not choose Abram for an exclusionary blessing, but in choosing Abram, he was choosing all of humanity, including those not yet within his covenant.

Later, within the Levitical laws, God's grace to strangers seems quite remarkable: "When foreigners reside among you in your land, do not mistreat them. The foreigners residing among you must be treated as your native-born. Love them as yourself, for you were foreigners in Egypt. I am the LORD your God" (Leviticus 19:33 – 34).

God went so far as to establish Levitical cities and cities of refuge as places where strangers could find justice and mercy:

> "Speak to the Israelites and say to them: 'When you cross the Jordan into Canaan, select some towns to be your cities of refuge, to which a person who has killed someone accidentally may flee. They will be places of refuge from the avenger, so that anyone accused of murder may not die before standing trial before the assembly.... These six towns will be a place of refuge for Israelites and for foreigners residing among them, so that anyone who has killed another accidentally can flee there.'"
>
> **Numbers 35:10 – 15**

Furthermore, the accused "are to stay in that city until they have stood trial before the assembly and until the death of the high priest who is serving at that time. Then they may go back to their own home in the town from which they fled" (Joshua 20:6). Strangers accused of murder were not only welcome to live in these cities; they also had the freedom to return to their homes once they were found innocent and enough time had passed.

Even in ancient times, when "human rights" were never considered, God introduced a process that allowed even the most despicable people a chance to be seen as "innocent until proven guilty." To a stranger accused of murder, the person to whom we would least likely desire to show mercy or kindness, God provides refuge. These cities of refuge, along with all cities of the Levites, offered compassion, justice, and mercy — even to the stranger.

When the Israelites asked God whether they should continue their fasting tradition, God concluded that he wanted something else from them: "This is what the LORD Almighty said: 'Administer true justice; show mercy and compassion to one another. Do not oppress the widow or the fatherless, the foreigner or the poor. Do not plot evil against each other'" (Zechariah 7:9 – 10). Sadly, the people refused to pay attention, which led to an ironic turn of events: they were soon dispersed and became strangers in strange lands (see verses 11 – 14).

Hospitality is lived out as we welcome and love strangers. The related word "hospice" originally referred to "a rest house for travelers" and conveys "a safe place." Our homes, our businesses, and our churches should become safe places for strangers, where they can experience kindness and love.

JESUS PARTIES

A party theology involves not only sending invitations but accepting invitations as well. Jesus seemed to have a negative reputation among the religious leaders, who called him "a glutton and a drunkard, a friend of tax collectors and sinners" (Matthew 11:19). His first miracle involved turning water into really good wine at a wedding party in Cana (see John 2). Jesus spent time speaking in synagogues and going to the temple in Jerusalem, but most of his best interactions took place in people's homes and in places near the Sea of Galilee, as well as when he was just walking along the way. Jesus' reputation came from his willingness to go to the places he was invited — the places where the best conversations could take place.

In the days when I served with a youth group in Seattle, Christy, a girl new to our community, invited us to her sixteenth birthday party — an invitation she issued in passing as she left an event one night, which made it seem almost like an afterthought. As the day approached, Debbie felt we should go, thinking it would be a great way to get to know Christy and her parents. Christy's dad was the one who first took her to our youth events, much to the displeasure of her mom, who didn't want Christy to have anything to do with church. Nonetheless, into this hostile environment we decided to enter. Filling our car with three teenagers, we drove to the skating rink and arrived just a few minutes late. Balloons, streamers, and cake decorated this festive moment. Though we assumed other guests were on the way, since the table was set for thirty people, we were still a bit surprised that when we walked in, we were the only people there besides Christy and her parents. Thirty minutes passed, and then an hour, but no one else showed up for the party. (Three kids did breeze in, but only to wish her a happy birthday on their way to another event.) I remember looking at Debbie in the middle of this party and thanking her for insisting that we come and being so grateful that we had brought three other people with us.

By the end of the night, we all had a blast playing video games, falling on the ice as we skated around together, and eating cake. (Man, we he had a lot of cake that night!) Most important, I will never forget the response of her family. A few weeks later, Julie, Christy's mom, the same mom who had harassed and berated her for coming to church, sat on the couch in the youth lounge, tears streaming down her face. Julie had decided to follow Christ. Curious about the reason for the dramatic turnaround, I asked Julie what had happened to move her from mocking Christy for her involvement at our church to now desiring this same relationship. Through her tears she looked at me and Debbie and revealed, "I changed my mind about God and Christians because you came to my daughter's party."

Stunned and silent, I thanked God that we had not missed this moment. In fact, it has changed the way we view invitations from those around us. If we receive an invitation from someone to see their school play and it happens to be the same night as our small group, not only do we miss the small group, but we also invite the small group to join us. We need to say no more often to our busyness so that we can create room for spontaneous adventures with others. We need to look for those who need a hug. We need to turn off our televisions and spend time in coffee shops. Ultimately, we need to reorient our lives so that we begin to invest in the people we already know and start investing in people who need a friend.

FIELD NOTES

I was never a huge fan of parties until I threw one.

After attending over a dozen weddings one year, a thought slammed into my mind. What would it look like if we put just as much time, energy, and maybe even money into celebrating something besides the love of two people (as great as that is)? What if churches and Christ-followers intentionally created events and experiences that were not merely for ourselves or for enhancing our agendas, but simply because life was worth celebrating?

So I put on my brand-new party planner hat and started planning the best party I could imagine.

I wanted a party that was radically inclusive, provocative, and meaningful. While I could have easily acquired a church building at no charge, religious spaces don't usually scream inclusiveness. I looked into renting art galleries but they were quoting prices in the range of $20,000 (which I think was their way of saying no). I ended up cold-calling a nightclub manager, pitching my vision and walking out with the venue and staff for free, along with a wonderful friendship.

Once I had secured the club, people realized I was dead serious about the party extravaganza. Plenty of friends came out of the woodwork to volunteer to help. Everyone I knew became a talent scout and was empowered to invite people to both come and contribute; this was going to be a party for everyone. I'm tone-deaf and know nothing about music, but artists began sending me their albums and demo tracks weekly for review. It's amazing how much undiscovered talent is all around us; sometimes people just need an excuse to showcase it.

We also decided up front that while we were going to have a cover charge for the party, we would give 100 percent of the proceeds toward building a well and providing clean water to those who need it most. We wanted not only to provide a spectacular night of community and creativity but also to inform people and urge them to get involved in a worthwhile cause.

And what a party it was! Hundreds of people from all sorts of cultures, faiths, and backgrounds gathered to celebrate and be inspired by music, dance, fashion, paint, and photography. Everyone was invited to leave a mark through collaborative art projects. Different social networks and circles of friends converged and interacted. Even a dude I just met earlier selling graffiti T-shirts on the street came because he wanted to be a part of "something bigger" for a night.

Was the name of Jesus explicitly proclaimed at any time during the party? Nope. But was Jesus encountered through the conversations, the creativity, and the community? Absolutely. Parties may seem secular to most, but they can be profoundly sacred if you treat them as so.

We've since had more parties, and what's even more exciting is seeing people who didn't get why we were having a party fall in love with the idea and spin off Christ-inspired parties of their own. They don't need to be large or elaborate in any way, just intentional.

Parties aren't essential to life, but they surely do make life a lot more joy filled. Wouldn't it be amazing for people to see that Jesus compels us toward hope and celebration that tangibly spills over into our communities?

People are longing for someone, especially a friend, to do something out of the ordinary that they can become a part of. Our world is desperately in need of spaces that create meaningful connections. Throw parties; they can change everything.

Lon Wong

Lon is a husband, father, missionary, social media junkie, and lover of jalapeños and cheddar. Lon lives in Toronto, Ontario, Canada, and can be found online at *www.solarcrash.com*.

Chapter 4

A FELLOWSHIP OF FREAKS

Finding a Common Cause to Create Community

Have you ever found yourself insulated from the world around you, stuck in a Christian bubble? Working, meeting, serving, and playing with fellow Christians had become the norm for me. The time came when I knew I had to think through my options for developing new and genuine friendships with others. I considered joining a gym, sports league, or a service organization, or even taking some classes at a nearby university. Those options seemed to require too much sweat, time, and money. So I chose the next most logical place to connect with new friends: I decided to become a stand-up comic.

I imagine there are other comedians out there who work at a church by day and hit the comedy clubs and coffee bars at night.

Since I speak often and occasionally share a humorous anecdote or two, I assumed the transition would be simple. How naive and wrong I was! Standing in front of a crowd of strangers who have gathered for the express purpose of laughing is actually quite horrifying. Making people laugh at church is relatively easy. They tend to know you already, so they'll laugh at anything even mildly amusing. Men and women in a coffee shop or a comedy club are not nearly as easily amused. I discovered that you actually have to be funny, which requires writing fresh material and delivering jokes that make people laugh. Have you ever tried to amuse someone when they are waiting to laugh? Most of the time we get people to laugh by saying something funny when they aren't expecting it. As a stand-up comedian, you have to deliver something hilarious every thirty seconds just to keep the audience's attention.

As I began to connect with other comics and work on my act at a few coffee shops and bars, I discovered something very interesting. Though comics seem cynical and miserable during their acts, they truly *are* cynical and miserable. It's not an act! I would warn my friends who would come to cheer me on that most of the other comics weren't as clean as I was. I discovered this the hard way after inviting a friend and his twelve-year-old daughter to a show. Even though the comedy club said that twelve-year-olds were welcome to come, that didn't mean they should. The first comic was so taken aback that a young girl was sitting in the front row that she seemed to get more and more nasty with her material, even addressing my friend's daughter, a child who was being home-schooled, with, "So, have you ever met a lesbian before?" I was extremely embarrassed as my friend and his daughter snuck out after the first act, which had been foul, rude, and crude. Another time, when my wife, Debbie, was there with me, a guy decided to flirt with her during his act. When I say "flirt," I really mean that he pulled up his shirt and rubbed his hairy stomach up and down her back.

After doing a show with a few comics who had gotten airtime on commercials and on NBC's *Last Comic Standing* (ironically, there were twelve performers but only fifteen total people in the room), I gave my phone number to a comic with whom I had really clicked, hoping that we'd be able to work on some material together. As he was looking for his card, he asked me what I did for a living, since almost all of the comics in my world have other jobs as they try to make it big. I paused for a moment and admitted that I worked at a church called Mosaic. Suddenly he stopped looking around in his computer bag. He looked me in the eye and said, "I can't find my card, but I'll give you a call so we can write stuff together." As you can imagine, I never heard from him again.

After months and months of trying to befriend other comics without any success, I was ready to retire. The awkward moments and bad nights on stage weren't worth the trouble. Just before ending my comedy career completely, a fellow comic named Allan Flowers invited me to lunch. Allan would always see to it that I'd be able to get on stage at any of the shows he was hosting. He was always one of the funniest comics, and his material was really smart and clean. Allan worked at Fox Studios behind the scenes on shows like *Best Damn Sports Show Period*. One day, after clearing security at Fox, I met Allan, who gave me a tour and took me to lunch. During our conversation about comedy and life, I realized I may not be a comic forever, but I never want to miss genuine friendships with people, no matter where they are on their spiritual journey. The "abuse" and challenges I faced were worth it if in the process I could gain friends like Allan.

FINDING A CAUSE

To move out of our rut and routine, we should look to connect with others through a cause, hobby, or area of passion. Whether we are drawn toward skateboarding, gardening, homeless ministry, reading, a particular support group, sports, theater, or whatever it may be, we should seek to unite with others in those communities as a way to build new relationships.

The majority of Jesus' most important moments in his ministry involved places away from the temple. Whether he was walking through the countryside on his way to a town, celebrating a religious holiday, enjoying dinner with friends at someone's house, attending a wedding, or whatever he might be doing, Jesus developed relationships and served people away from the religious buildings around him, outside of the synagogues or temple. For Jesus, serving the Father meant getting involved in the lives of others. Too often we get so involved in our churches that we get stuck inside church buildings, unable to see the people outside who need us.

For Debbie and me, having children has opened up new relationships with lots of great new friends. Once you have a child, there is no cause more uniting than parenting. When I see another dad at the mall whose little girl is screaming for a piece of candy, I feel his pain. Without even saying a word, I look to make eye contact with the beleaguered dad. When he sees me pushing my daughter in her stroller, we connect. He knows I know what he is experiencing. When he sees my four-year-old, Trevi, sitting calmly, it gives him hope that his two-year-old won't always behave in the way she's behaving at that moment.

Our first experience with this quick connection among parents took place before our son was even born. Debbie insisted we attend

Lamaze classes. Admittedly, I was extremely reluctant. We had seen enough childbirth reenactments on television and in the movies, so I figured I knew enough already. The woman screams and pushes, while the guy holds her hand and avoids watching. When we arrived at the first class, my fears of boredom and embarrassment came true. The teacher spent a great deal of time sharing with us things we already knew, and we had to make strange sounds publicly. To make matters worse, all of the couples seemed to keep to themselves.

Before our second class, I couldn't hold in my frustration any longer. I mentioned to the guy next to me what a horrific experience this was for me. Just as quickly as I began to vent, he turned to me and shared sentiments very similar to mine. Soon another guy joined in with his reasons for trying to skip the class. While the guys began to commiserate, the women started huddling together to complain about the guys. The room filled with excited voices — men complaining about the class, and women complaining about the men who were complaining about the class. Over the next several weeks, we enjoyed getting to know some of the other couples during dinner before class or dessert afterward. We remained in contact for several months as our new friends began having their babies. We've maintained a close friendship with one couple even to this day.

Through our kids, we have met many remarkable and amazing people at preschool, kindergarten, T-ball games, and in the neighborhood. Some have remained lasting friends who continue to bless our lives. Others have taken steps to connect or reconnect with Christ through our encouragement. Parenting opens up hearts and minds to the possibility of a loving God for those who have yet to believe. Pregnancy, childbirth, and then the act of holding a new little life shows the magnificent creation of God. Sleepless nights, tantrums, and toilet training show that we need God to survive.

CAUSE CREATES COMMUNITY

We often find ourselves connecting with others we never even would have met had we not been in the same band, play, or football team. When we pursue the same cause, our shared experiences and shared goals bring us together.

Avid sports fans often debate whether good chemistry creates a winning team or whether a winning team creates good chemistry. As the debate rages on, one thing we know: chemistry and winning are connected. Good chemistry and a winning team both have a common cause at their origin. Living in Los Angeles, I have seen this repeatedly during basketball season.

I can't stand the Lakers. After cheering for the Dallas Mavericks and the Seattle SuperSonics for so many years, I just can't bring myself to give the Lakers my allegiance. You would think that I would be swayed by their ability to win and the fact that they have a star player with the last name Bryant, but instead I choose to cheer for the Clippers. I have to admit, the Clippers have been hard to support. Year after year, their best players leave for new teams. I am jeered at and laughed at by other sports fans, yet I proudly wear my Clippers gear. In spite of the criticism, and even when the Lakers won three championships in a row (2000 – 2002) while the Clippers failed to make the playoffs, I did not waver.

Now, finally, after not winning a playoff series in thirty years, the Clippers have shown signs of marked improvement. Could the Clippers be on the verge of their own basketball dynasty, perhaps even eclipsing the Lakers in popularity? Will Jack Nicholson trade in his courtside seats at Lakers games to cheer on the Clippers?

Thinking back to the Lakers prior to their championship run gives me hope. The Lakers endured some difficult days as well. Sure, it wasn't thirty years of losing, but there were several seasons when Kobe Bryant and Shaquille O'Neal fought more than they won. After Phil Jackson arrived, something changed. Seeing Shaq talk with the media before that first championship season in 2000 intrigued me. Rather than his usual comical proclamations about how great he was or how smart he was, he seemed to sincerely announce his focus on winning a championship. Repeatedly, he assured the interviewers that nothing else mattered but winning the championship.

Throughout the season, the usual sniping between Kobe and Shaq dissipated. Instead, the entire team seemed to play together on both ends of the court. After Kobe had been suspended for a game, Shaq came out of the locker room wearing a Kobe jersey to show his support. Several times throughout the season and the playoffs, these two men, who seemingly despised each other, would huddle up together, cheer each other on, and even slap each other on the butt. In the process, the cause of winning the championship galvanized their relationship and created community and camaraderie.

Jesus' cause created community in his day. I doubt that Peter the fisherman and Matthew the tax collector ever would have been friends if not for their common cause — to become "fishers of people." Jesus chose an unusually diverse group to follow him. Instead of choosing men who were respected by others because of their professions (i.e., rabbis, lawyers, politicians, etc.), Jesus chose fishermen, a tax collector, and a zealot. By joining Jesus' small group, this motley crew of men became friends. They had nicknames for each other, such as "the Rock" and "Sons of Thunder." They traveled together for several years, and in the end, they were imprisoned and willingly went to their deaths for their leader.

Jesus began his revolution with a simple invitation: "Come, follow me, and I will send you out to fish for people" (Matthew 4:19).

He invited this unlikely group to lose their lives in serving others. Contrary to what we would expect, Jesus did not invite them to follow him so that he could teach them the Scriptures, answer their prayers, meet their needs, or even take them to heaven. Jesus led the greatest small group in history because he was more than a Bible study leader or prayer group facilitator. Jesus was a revolutionary. His small group gathered together to feed the five thousand. His small group went on field trips to exorcise demons and perform miracles. After Jesus' death and resurrection, Jesus' small group changed the world.

Jesus' eternal cause also creates a diverse community. A community on a mission to love and serve its city becomes diverse through the natural connections of relationships. At Mosaic, for example, we have seen homosexuals, followers of Hare Krishna, Scientologists, agnostics, Buddhists, Muslims, secularists, Democrats, Republicans, Socialists, Libertarians, children, adults, senior adults, entire extended families, and even "Christians" choose to follow Christ. How does this happen? These men and women from diverse backgrounds are all relationally connected to someone who goes to our church. The people we befriend will be the people we reach. We are not targeting people because of their heritage. We are trying to love, serve, and reach our friends, who just happen to be named Javier, Sandeep, Pam, Hwee Ching, and Molene.

Plagued by insecurities, feeling like an outcast, and deeply desiring to find God, a young woman mentioned to her friend that she wanted to find a church that "caters to the freaks of Los Angeles." Her friend decided she needed to visit Mosaic. As a freak myself who felt welcomed immediately by our community, I understood why her friend brought her to Mosaic. Our very name — Mosaic — represents the many broken and fragmented people whom God has brought together to create a beautiful picture.

We all have "freakish" moments, times when we sense we just don't fit in, times when we feel relationally disconnected and awkward. Our churches need to actively engage and welcome those around us, including "freaks," into our fellowship.

For many of us, our cause remains too small. Survival binds some of our churches together, yet in order to thrive we must change our priorities. When our cause focuses inward, we develop unhealthy relationships. Like kissing cousins, we feel close to our family, yet no one else feels welcomed or comfortable. As guests come and then go, we end up missing out on the opportunity to learn from new relationships.

When our cause focuses on those not yet in our community, everyone enjoys a more pleasant and loving environment. Communities that welcome guests with open arms reveal themselves to be warmer places.

Unfortunately, in our culture, the term "fellowship" has come to imply a mushy, hand-holding, campfire, "kumbaya" moment, yet the Scriptures translate the word as "a partnership in a cause" (see Philippians 1:6). The recently revived Lord of the Rings trilogy helps reframe the true meaning of this word — a cause that unites a variety of people (or in this case, creatures). If hobbits, a dwarf, elves, and even a couple of humans who share animosity toward each other can partner together for the task of destroying a ring, then certainly we can become a fellowship of freaks, whose cause remains the most important mission in history.

FUSION

Serving as a catalyst (that is, youth pastor) with teenagers in East Los Angeles helped me discover the power of connecting people to the cause of Christ. People long to be part of something important. I remember asking one of the girls in our youth group what she hoped to do for her career after she graduated. She replied, "I want to be an activist, but I just don't know for what."

Connecting to a cause rather than building convictions within people seems to have longer lasting effects. So many teens believe the right things, only to fall away once they graduate from high school and go on to college. Those who have been actively serving and reaching out have a better chance of staying connected in the days ahead of them.

Maria had been involved in our youth ministry for several years. She was a very sharp young woman with big dreams. As a senior in high school, she was very involved at school and somewhat faithful to our youth group. When we invited Maria in the spring of 2000 to serve as part of Fusion, our outreach-oriented small groups, we could sense the tension. She was reluctant to be more involved at first, but she truly desired to help her friends spiritually.

At first, no one came to the small group other than Maria and my wife, Debbie. Weeks went by without any of her friends coming. She would invite them, but they weren't interested. During one of those nights when no on else came, Maria confessed to Debbie that she had been sleeping with her boyfriend and needed help. Later we walked her and her boyfriend through a process to help them in this area. They broke up, got involved in different ministries, and shared with their parents about their struggles.

Soon Maria began asking Debbie lots of questions about the Scriptures. She really wanted to know what God thought about the issues young women face in high school — temptations, trials, and so on. Eventually, a few of her friends began to come to the group. Not long after that, Maria helped lead five of her friends to faith in Christ.

Amazed by the turn of events, I asked Maria what had happened. She shared her frustration about inviting her friends to Fusion but none of them being interested enough to show up. They would ask, "Why should we come?" When she'd mention how God could change their lives, they responded by saying, "Well, he hasn't changed yours." It was in this context that she shared with Debbie about her struggles with her boyfriend. Seeing her break up with her boyfriend and noticing the changes in the way she was living, her friends began asking her questions about God. Not knowing how to answer them, Maria began asking Debbie questions about the Scriptures. Soon her friends wanted to find what she now obviously had — a life-transforming relationship with God.

Once Maria committed to the cause of Christ, she realized that her life didn't match her beliefs. How could she share with her friends about the life-changing power of God when she wasn't allowing God to change *her*? Even though I had shared with the teens the importance of sexual purity and challenged them to read the Scriptures, none of this mattered to Maria until she became more concerned about her friends than about herself. Connecting to the cause of Christ guided her through her moral struggles and even pulled her into the Scriptures. By attempting to help change the lives of her friends, her life was changed.

Jesus began a small group with a focus on outreach. In fact, at one point, Jesus sent his small group out on an intriguing mission. Matthew writes about it:

> He called his twelve disciples to him and gave them authority to drive out evil spirits and to heal every disease and sickness. . . .
> These twelve Jesus sent out with the following instructions:

"Do not go among the Gentiles or enter any town of the Samaritans. Go rather to the lost sheep of Israel. As you go, proclaim this message: 'The kingdom of heaven has come near.' Heal the sick, raise the dead, cleanse those who have leprosy, drive out demons. Freely you have received, freely give."

Matthew 10:1 , 5–8

After Jesus explained this unusual small group activity, he warned the disciples that they would be persecuted, challenged, and mocked. I thought Jesus loved these men — so why would he knowingly place them in harm's way without enough supplies or training? We discover a powerful principle in the midst of Jesus' instructions and warnings. Jesus tells them, "Whoever finds their life will lose it, and whoever loses their life for my sake will find it" (Matthew 10:39).

Christ's cause changes our lives as we seek to help others change as well. Jesus knew that his followers would carry his message after his death. Rather than merely spending time discussing the Scriptures and praying, he created opportunities for his small group to put their faith into action. Can you imagine what their next debriefing with Jesus would have been like after these guys had come face-to-face with demons? I expect they decided they had better take lots of notes now as Jesus talked — knowing they needed to be better prepared for the next small-group adventures Jesus had in mind for them. Jesus invested in his small group by discussing the Scriptures, praying, developing authentic relationships, and sending them out to serve others. Our faith grows when we have to actually use it. We learn more when we teach others. Serving others changes us.

We were created to do something significant with our lives. To influence people toward a commitment to Christ, we should find other causes that will result in dynamic new and developing relationships, and when we connect others with the cause of Christ, we connect to the most important mission of all.

FIELD NOTES

What I love about this chapter is that Eric is going against the grain of church culture. Too often we promote "fellowship" and "community" in our churches in ways that foster narcissism because it ends up being all about us. If we turn our fellowship into being together on a mission, it becomes something entirely different than sitting in a fellowship hall eating donuts and hanging out as we talk about the latest sermon or Christian CD we listened to. Just as in the example Eric gave of the *Fellowship of the Ring*, in which various types of people come together, fellowship becomes a missional adventure. Community is still "fellowship," but now it results in praying for one another and caring for one another as you serve Jesus on a mission.

The point isn't just to be in a cozy community; it is about supporting each other while on a mission to serve the world like Jesus would want us to. We need to be healthy disciples of Jesus on a mission, which is why we need each other. But without the mission part, we can easily become passive spectators who sit around with each other in "community," and it becomes more about us than it does about others who desperately need to know and experience the love and grace of Jesus and the beauty of knowing him.

As this chapter begins, Eric talks about taking specific action to get out of the church world and into the real world. For him it was becoming involved in stand-up comedy. What are the things you find interesting that could propel you into the world to meet people like Eric did?

The longer we are Christians, the fewer non-Christians we hang out with. Look back on the past week or two. How much social engagement have you had with Christians in comparison to those who don't know Jesus yet?

If you are going out with church friends — to movies or whatever you may be doing socially — can you think of those who are not part of your church, or who haven't yet experienced positive examples of Christians, that you could invite to come with you? I believe the most powerful form of evangelism is simply hanging out with people and being their friend. Through time spent together and the building up of trust, the gospel will be talked about somehow. People — if they are your friends — will desire to know about your church community if it is important in your life. But instead of having another Friday night with Christians, why not invite people out of your normal Christian circles to join you in seeing a movie. No weird or awkward discussions. Just hanging out. And then see what God does over time. It transforms a normal Friday night at the movie theatre into holy ground as you represent Jesus to those who may not know him (yet).

Dan Kimball

Dan is the author of *They Like Jesus but Not the Church* and is a teaching pastor at Vintage Faith Church in Santa Cruz, California, as well as being on the leadership team of Origins (*www.origins project.org*). Dan blogs at *www.dankimball.com*.

Part
2

LOVE IS
THE NEW
APOLOGETIC

Chapter 5

UNCIVIL WAR

Proving That God Is Real

"I know what all of you are thinking, but I am not the devil."

That thought had never crossed my mind.

But now I began to wonder.

Debbie and I had been invited by a good friend to join him in planting a church in Seattle, Washington, and our move was filled with great expectations. We saw ourselves as part of the team that would create "the Saddleback of Seattle" or "the Willow Creek of the Northwest." My dad tried to dissuade us from making such a drastic move after just two months of marriage by reminding us that more people attempted suicide in Seattle than in any other city in the country. These facts attracted rather than repelled us. We wanted to move to the great Northwest to bring light into a place known for darkness.

Seattle is one of the most depressing yet also one of the most beautiful places in the world. The sun never peeks through the dark, low-lying clouds of winter, while the drizzle continually moistens the sky and ground; in the summer, however, the sun appears just after 5:00 a.m. and doesn't sleep until almost 10:00 p.m. People emerge from their caves and holes of hibernation to hike, bike, run, swim, and do just about anything that can be done outdoors.

Our Seattle plan involved starting a seeker-sensitive church called "The Anchor." We were geared up to do a Thursday night event for seekers and a large group Bible study for Christians on Sunday nights. We met in the same building as Brookhaven Baptist Church, a group made up of about twelve senior adults who met on Sunday mornings. Our friend Norm attempted to lead both congregations while we assembled a dream team of leaders with the help of outside donors. If our plan came together, we would grow fast enough that we would no longer need gifts from others outside of our church in order to afford salaries for three pastors, a receptionist, and eventually me, though at first I would volunteer as the student ministry leader while holding down a job in the real world.

Many great things happened at The Anchor. With talented singers, speakers, leaders, musicians, and greeters on board, we seemed positioned for great things. Unfortunately, the pace of growth did not meet our expectations. Our weekly seeker event called "Seen It, Done It, Been There" failed to draw people to see it, do it, or even be there. As a result, we made a desperate and, in retrospect, unfortunate decision: we combined The Anchor and Brookhaven Baptist Church.

The merger soon polarized our community to the point that each side saw itself as fighting for God and the other group as fighting against God. In reality, we were trying to combine two very different visions. And this is the context in which a seventy-year-old Baptist deacon stood to remind us — at a church business meeting — that he was not the lord of the underworld.

"I am not the devil."

I had always pictured the devil to have the stereotypical red skin, red eyes, crazy black hair, black goatee, horns, tail — you know, like the devil we see walking around at Halloween. I had never imagined he might take a more human form, especially not the form of a gentle, thin, gray-haired seventy-year-old Baptist deacon. How could we have come to the place where people who believed in Jesus had to clarify that they were not actually the incarnational version of Satan himself? How could people who are supposed to be known by their love hate each other so much?

In this particular situation, this group — the "Brookhaven Twelve," as we called them — had paved the way for the launch of several churches over the years in the Seattle area, not just The Anchor. Their tenacity and perseverance even to hang on to a church building near Lake Washington with only twelve people in attendance was truly admirable. Many others would have closed the doors under far less trying circumstances.

As Brookhaven dissolved into The Anchor and the praise music with drums and guitar replaced the hymns with piano and organ, we began to see the downside of this quality of tenacity and perseverance. These men and women *never give up*, and they weren't about to do so now that their way of "doing church" was threatened. A fine line exists between being persistent and persevering and being stubborn.

During services one Sunday morning, an irate gentleman stood up and hastily fled the auditorium. Following him to see if I could help with whatever was troubling him, I found him just outside the doors. With fire in his eyes and rage in his voice, he declared, "This is why God destroyed Sodom and Gomorrah!" Not having seen anyone being raped or other acts of immorality taking place inside, I asked for clarification. "It's the electric guitars and drums! This is an abomination!" Since I had not yet started my seminary training, I wasn't completely positive, but I didn't think God smote Sodom and Gomorrah because they were using electric guitars in their worship. With the advent of electricity coming several millennia later, I was confused, until he warned me before stomping away, "God does not like improper worship!"

Another time, a generally sweet and reserved woman flipped out on David, one of our leaders, after she discovered that we had sold the pews from the chapel, a room seldom used at that point. She was so furious that we would sell these precious pews that she screamed at him, "Pastors come and go, but pews are forever!" We weren't too shocked by her response in the midst of the other confrontations and heated conversations, but we *had* been surprised someone would actually pay us money for used pews.

Both sides drew lines in the sand, with the only conversations between each other taking place in business meetings. Each group was waiting for the other to give up, until everyone was exhausted and distracted from our true purpose — making and growing disciples, and loving outsiders and loving each other. Instead of uniting around a common cause to reach Seattle with the good news about Jesus, we were fractured and fighting for control and for the right to set the direction of the church.

FINDING PEACE

The one time in history when Jesus prayed for you and for me, he prayed that we would live at peace with each other. Our relationships with each other affect other people's relationship with God. Jesus prayed, speaking first of his disciples and then of us:

> My prayer is not for them alone. I pray also for those who will believe in me through their message, that all of them may be one, Father, just as you are in me and I am in you. May they also be in us so that the world may believe that you have sent me. I have given them the glory that you gave me, that they may be one as we are one — I in them and you in me — so that they may be brought to complete unity. Then the world will know that you sent me and have loved them even as you have loved me.
>
> John 17:20 – 23

Jesus wants our lives to be so transformed that we actually care for those around us and that the love we share for each other bubbles over into the lives of those not yet following Christ. Our love for others proves that God is real. Our love for other followers of Christ helps those who do not follow Christ trust God. No pressure, huh? Hostility and conflict within the church undermine our efforts to show the world God's grace and love. Why would those outside the church have any interest in connecting with us when all they see is our conflict? Most people have enough conflict in their own lives without seeing it played out at church.

In addition to the great and inspiring moments that occurred in the early church, we also read about a great deal of heresy, immorality, and conflict. Paul and Barnabas chose to separate over a difference in opinion about one of their traveling companions, Mark (see Acts 15:36 – 41). Paul and Peter disagreed about how to treat Gentiles (see Galatians 2:11 – 14). Another time, Paul and Peter united to go against the Judaizers (see Acts 15:7 – 11). As I mentioned earlier, Judaizers wanted Gentiles to become Jewish before they could become followers of Christ. Looking at how the early church resolved this controversial issue reveals that a church *can* work through genuine and deep differences in a loving and civil way.

The story from Acts 15 reveals a great deal of "sharp dispute and debate" (verse 2) among the opposing sides; as a result, leaders from each side were appointed to present their side to the apostles and elders in Jerusalem. Both groups respectfully allowed the other to make their argument: "The whole assembly became silent as they listened ..." (Acts 15:12). Both sides appealed to the Scriptures, but Barnabas, Paul, and Peter also shared personal stories about their supernatural experiences and interactions with Gentiles who were choosing to follow Christ. Both groups allowed for a process of mediation with those in authority in their lives. James, who also referred to the Scriptures, offered a solution: "It is my judgment, therefore, that we should not make it difficult for the Gentiles who are turning to God. Instead we should write to them, telling them to abstain from food polluted by idols, from sexual immorality, from the meat of strangled animals and from blood" (Acts 15:19 – 20). With the decision made, the leaders chose some representatives to share with the Gentile believers their decision in person and in writing.

Resolving this conflict required both sides to make the effort to travel to another place for mediation and to trust the decision made. In our conflicts, we need to examine the Scriptures to give us guidance — looking at similar experiences in the lives of others as well as the character of God. Since both sides had Scriptures that could back their cause, in the end, the decision was made with eyes focused on the outsider. When in doubt, we should make decisions to help those who are being overlooked or disenfranchised. Our decisions should come down on the side of showing love to the immature believer or the nonbeliever. Those who are most mature in Christ need to be willing to make the greatest sacrifices.

Jesus acknowledged that conflict among believers is inevitable, and he encourages us to work out our conflict within the church rather than pursuing lawsuits against each other in the courts (see Matthew 5:25). He went on to teach that we should even be OK if we get ripped off: "If anyone wants to sue you and take your shirt, hand over your coat as well" (Matthew 5:40).

Paul offers similar insights in a letter he wrote to a church embroiled in conflict — the church in Corinth:

> If any of you has a dispute with another, do you dare to take it before the ungodly for judgment instead of before the Lord's people?... Therefore, if you have disputes about such matters, do you ask for a ruling from those whose way of life is scorned in the church? I say this to shame you. Is it possible that there is nobody among you wise enough to judge a dispute between believers? But instead, one brother goes to law against another — and this in front of unbelievers!
>
> The very fact that you have lawsuits among you means you have been completely defeated already. Why not rather be wronged? Why not rather be cheated?
>
> **1 Corinthians 6:1, 4 – 7**

If living in peace together seems beyond reach, going in different directions while respecting each other remains an acceptable option as well. Just after Paul and Barnabas worked through the conflict with the Judaizers, they had a disagreement that led them to go their separate ways. Even godly people disagree. Ironically, they chose not to bring in an arbitrator, perhaps knowing that in this case, two teams were better than just one.

As frail and fragile human beings, we will have conflict, yet many of our conflicts would be resolved within our churches if we resolved to sit down together, talk things through, listen to each other, make sacrifices for the sake of those furthest from God, and, when necessary, listen to a mediator. We can resolve corporate conflict in our churches by applying principles used in solving interpersonal conflict. We are to seek to live in peace with our "brothers and sisters" in our church family, just as we must in our birth family. We should strive to become places of peace — both personal and corporate — so that we may show God's transforming power.

CLOSE CONFLICT

Often our most bitter battles are with those we love. I typically don't yell at my coworkers at the office or snap at a grocery store clerk. Instead, I have had my greatest tirades with my brother and parents, or my wife and children. Why is that? How can we so quickly turn on those we love? Perhaps because it is in those relationships that we are living out who we truly are. We're just being ourselves. In public, we put on our best face and practice our best behavior, yet when we are at home our true character breaks through the surface.

In the fall of 2005, I was doing a series on the topic "Beyond Ordinary" at one of Mosaic's weekly gatherings. We were tackling issues such as extraordinary service, extraordinary love, and extraordinary ambition, while each week, Debbie and I were struggling through extraordinary conflict.

Usually our fights began over the silliest issues: "Why didn't you call me to let me know what time you were coming home?" "Why did you order that boba tea and not get me the kind I like?" "Why did you leave the water running while you were brushing your teeth?" I'm not exactly sure why I became so quickly frustrated with Debbie, but on one particular day my angry comments failed to elicit an angry response from her. She decided to ignore my ranting. That made me even more upset. For several hours I refused to talk with Debbie, and she was just fine with not talking with me.

Thinking somehow that the kids could have fun, even as we were making each other miserable, we took them to the zoo in the midst of our feud. As Debbie and the kids wandered around in the bat cave, I sat in the stroller with my arms folded and a scowl on my face. Children and their parents were playing and walking around as I was sitting there stewing in my anger. I noticed several moms and dads whisk their kids away as they saw me sitting in a dark corner in that stroller. I was so angry with Debbie that I didn't care what I looked like or who I scared.

As I sat there, I dreamed of ways to prolong the silence for days or even weeks, yet Debbie's refusal to give in to my demands to apologize forced my hand. I realized that *I* was at fault (as usual), and I began considering ways to end the fight without admitting any wrongdoing. I finally swallowed my pride and approached Debbie — who was standing behind one of the fake stalactites in the cave. The thought that I would be speaking the next day on the topic of "extraordinary contentment" spurred me to want to make things right with her.

If unresolved, conflict leads toward death — perhaps not in a physical sense, but in a spiritual sense. How many times have you and I allowed conflict to separate us from those we love? Death means separation. Physical death involves a separation of our spirit from our body. Spiritual death means a separation of our spirit from God. Relational death separates us from others. We allow even the smallest arguments and annoyances to move us toward "the silent treatment," acting as though the other person no longer exists. Some of us have even gone so far as to act as though the one we used to love is now "dead to us." We deem the person we hate as unworthy of our time, our attention, and our help. Rather than actively destroying someone, we act as though the person has already been destroyed.

Hatred reveals itself in the forms of slander, harsh comments, prejudice, rage, murder, negligence, bitterness, and broken relationships. Hatred acts like a pet pit bull. We like to bring it out to scare others away, not realizing that it could very well come back to bite us too. Hatred when unleashed in our lives destroys others and comes back to destroy us as well. Here's the thing, though: we do not have to give in to hatred. We can actually be known by our love, even when someone hurts us or annoys us or disagrees with us.

Cain's killing his brother Abel proves that proximity does not guarantee intimacy. When we give in to hatred, we follow Cain down a perilous path. Cain's life was overtaken by hatred and ended in isolation and restless wandering. Cain killed his brother, someone to whom he was close. They shared childhood together. They ran around the fields together. How could things have spiraled out of control so dramatically?

In the course of time Cain brought some of the fruits of the soil as an offering to the LORD. But Abel also brought an offering — fat portions from some of the firstborn of his flock. The LORD looked with favor on Abel and his offering, but on Cain and his offering he did not look with favor. So Cain was very angry, and his face was downcast.

Then the LORD said to Cain, "Why are you angry? Why is your face downcast? If you do what is right, will you not be accepted? But if you do not do what is right, sin is crouching at your door; it desires to have you, but you must rule over it."

Now Cain said to his brother Abel, "Let's go out to the field." While they were in the field, Cain attacked his brother Abel and killed him.

Then the LORD said to Cain, "Where is your brother Abel?" "I don't know," he replied. "Am I my brother's keeper?' "

Genesis 4:3 – 9

Cain stumbled down this road as a result of selfishness and displaced anger. Cain attempted to meet God on his own terms, and he was frustrated that he wasn't getting his way. In a demonstration of displaced anger, Cain killed his brother — when really he was angry with God. He was no longer his brother's keeper, and he saw others the way he saw himself. Hatred leads to isolation.

We avoid real relationships when we allow hatred to fester in our hearts. We conclude that *we* aren't worth loving, since we cannot see anyone else as worthy of our love. Our unwillingness to engage in the hard conversations or to receive a necessary rebuke in love keeps us from becoming better people.

Often our self-hatred results from the guilt we feel for choices we have made. We take out our personal frustrations on the people who happen to be right beside us. Our brokenness cuts those who try to get close.

Cain was flirting with disaster. He knew the right thing to do.

God warned him, yet he chose the wrong path. God chose both Cain and Abel, but Cain walked away. It's OK to get frustrated or even angry, yet we need to avoid allowing our anger to move us toward negative actions. At times in our lives, and even at different times during each day, we find ourselves at a fork in the road. We have the opportunity to take the path toward love, peace, and hope, or to follow the momentum of the world and culture around us and stumble on toward hatred and bitterness.

Peeking into King David's journal (aka "the Psalms"), we discover that "a man after God's own heart" (1 Samuel 13:14) is not immune to feelings of rage. How else can we explain David's prayer, where he seeks revenge on his enemies and asks God to "crush the heads of his enemies " so that the dogs have a chance to lick up the blood (Psalm 68:21, 23). As horrific as this sounds, David actually reveals a healthy way to handle frustration — venting with God.

After apologizing to Debbie at the zoo, I still had another important conversation to initiate. As we drove away, I silenced the VeggieTales music that was playing in the CD player.

"Kids, I'm really sorry I was mean to Mommy — will you forgive me?"

"Sure, if we can go back to the zoo."

"No, not today. Just don't ever treat Mommy the way I treated her."

I never want to have to say that again. I want my children to see a healthy relationship between their parents. Yes, we'll still get into arguments on occasion. Healthy relationships invariably experience conflict. If not, then there's a pretty good chance someone has just completely given up. We're human; we're going to have conflict. But how we negotiate through conflict will determine the type of people we become.

I love my wife and enjoy declaring my affection for her, but even if I proclaim my love to her out loud for all nearby pedestrians to hear as we stop at a traffic light, or scream, "I love you, Debbie!" as I jump up and down on the couch on the set of *The Oprah Winfrey Show*, how I treat her at home, in the car, or at the zoo is more important than what I could ever say about her publicly.

MAKING THINGS RIGHT

When we face conflict, we can choose to make the other person our enemy, or we can choose to make that person a friend by doing everything in our power to make sure that they know we love them. To ensure we live as peacemakers, Jesus gives us two different, seemingly contradictory commands. In one passage, Jesus says that the one offended should approach the one who did the offending; in another passage, Jesus declares that the one who has hurt someone should approach the one he offended. So which is it? Was Jesus confused?

According to Jesus, if someone hurts us, we should sit down in front of that person, face-to-face, to talk through what happened:

> If a brother or sister sins, go and point out the fault, just between the two of you. If they listen to you, you have won them over. But if they will not listen, take one or two others along, so that "every matter may be established by the testimony of two or three witnesses." If they still refuse to listen, tell it to the church; and if they refuse to listen even to the church, treat them as you would a pagan or a tax collector.
>
> **Matthew 18:15 – 17**

Notice that Jesus says nothing about email or voicemail. He doesn't mention anything about venting to as many people as possible about the heinous crimes committed against us. Jesus challenges us to actually sit down, face-to-face, with that person. If this approach doesn't work, then we get another person involved. Usually we will experience a renewed friendship somewhere within these first two steps. Just having another person in the room helps significantly, especially when the witness is someone both of the parties embroiled in the controversy have agreed to let in. Then, if this doesn't work, we need to involve others from our ministry. Generally, I try to involve a person's small group or ministry team, even before talking with the lead pastor or elders. Finally, if a conversation with ministry leaders fails to work, it is on this rare occasion, as an absolute last resort, that we would end our working relationship because of conflict.

Wouldn't you agree that much drama would be eliminated if we actually took Jesus' advice?

If reconciliation has not taken place after carefully following this process, then we should treat the offending person as someone who does not yet know Jesus. Ironically, this doesn't mean we excommunicate this person from our lives. The offending person may no longer have the same responsibilities with us, but if we are to treat him or her as a "pagan or tax collector," then we are to keep on loving *without conditions*. Jesus spent his time and energy interacting with pagans and tax collectors, loving and serving them.

Earlier in Matthew's gospel, Jesus speaks to crowds of people in his Sermon on the Mount. He declares here that if we hurt someone, we should sit down in front of that person, face-to-face, to talk through what happened: "If you are offering your gift at the altar and there remember that your brother of sister has something against you, leave your gift there in front of the altar. First go and be reconciled to that person; then come and offer your gift" (Matthew 5:23 – 24).

We see here that our relationship with God is affected by our relationship with people. Approaching a spiritually significant moment with God (offering a gift at an altar), we should be considering those we may have offended so we can go and make things right with them. If we don't, we won't be right with God.

Whether we have offended someone or have been offended by someone, in both cases, *we* are responsible for making things right. Jesus was not confused, nor was he contradictory. Jesus knew the tendencies of human nature, and he didn't want any of us to abdicate our responsibility to make peace with another person.

Even if we encounter someone who does not like us or someone who refuses to forgive us, we must make sure we have done everything in our power to move toward peace. Paul writes, "Let us therefore make every effort to do what leads to peace and to mutual edification" (Romans 14:19).

Tomorrow you might be the offender; the next day you might be the offended. In either case, as we live in this world of broken people, we have to learn to bring kindness to those who are hurting us and forgive those who anger us and violate us, and then to move to a place where we have done everything possible, "as far is it depends on [us]," to live in right relationships with one another — "to live at peace with everyone" (Romans 12:18).

I find great encouragement in Paul's use of the phrase "as far as it depends on [us]" when challenging us to live at peace with others. It is unfortunate, but there are times when no matter what we do, no matter how kind we've been or how hard we've tried to work things out, some people may refuse to forgive or to ask for forgiveness. In these extreme moments, we should pray for the miraculous and move on if we are sensing from God that we have, in fact, done all we could to promote peace.

When we follow Jesus' guidance in our relationships, we will be amazed at how many arguments can be resolved. Just sitting down face-to-face solves so much. So often our conflict is the result of a bad day on our part or the other person's part, a misunderstanding between us, or wrong assumptions held by one or the other or both.

I discovered this the hard way two days before Debbie and I got married. After spending the evening with my bride-to-be, I got back to my parents' house — the home where I had grown up — at about 11:00 p.m. After living away from my parents for several years, I was surprised that they were still awake at that late hour. I was even more surprised when I realized that they were upset at me because of my late arrival.

My dad began yelling at me for coming home so late and for not letting them know my plans. With the rehearsal dinner coming up the following night, they were still struggling to work out some of the details for that event. After my apologies were ignored and my parents continued to be frustrated, I decided to yell back at my dad. I planned to yell just once to get his attention, so we could continue the conversation at a lower decibel level. Unfortunately, once I started screaming, I couldn't stop. After volleying mean statements back and forth, we inched closer and closer to each other, fists clenched at our sides. My mom moved between us and shouted at both of us to stop. I wanted to punch my dad, but instead I left the living room.

And I plotted my revenge.

With our wedding and the move to Seattle drawing near, I decided that this would be the last conversation I would ever have with my dad. I would uninvite him to the wedding and the rehearsal dinner. At Christmas, only my mom would be invited. My future kids would never know their grandfather.

After several minutes, I began to come to my senses and decided to ask God for guidance in my response. I had avoided praying, because I knew what would happen — and I was right. As soon as I prayed, I felt like an idiot. My dad and I had had several skirmishes throughout the years, especially after the time I broke my brother's arm playing soccer, the time I poured gasoline into a Styrofoam cup in the garage, and the time I insisted on growing out my hair like a rock star, but this person *was* my dad. The same man who taught me to shave, drive a car, and work hard. This was the same man who served as a deacon at our church and took sermon tapes to those in the church who were too ill to attend worship on Sundays. This was the man who coached my Little League baseball team, took our family on vacations, and paid for me to go to college. Other fond memories about my dad flooded my mind.

Reluctantly and sheepishly, I walked to my parents' bedroom to ask my dad for his forgiveness. I hated to admit defeat, but I knew it was the right thing to do. The lights were out in their bedroom, and both of my parents were in bed. Kneeling at the side of the bed where my dad was lying, I heard something strange. My dad was crying.

My dad rarely cries. He has always been a man with a tough exterior. The only times I remember seeing or hearing my dad cry were at my grandfather's funeral and when Dad prayed publicly at church. (I am not sure why praying at church always seemed to trigger his tear ducts; perhaps he was moved by God's Spirit or was simply just freaking out as an introverted person forced to do something publicly that he considered quite private.)

Starting to get choked up myself, I mumbled out my apology. My dad then confessed the true reason for his frustration: he was having a hard time saying good-bye. In two days I would be married, and in two months I would be moving two thousand miles away. His anger was the result of feeling out of control and thinking about losing me.

I am so glad I decided to apologize to my dad that night rather than acting on my angry impulses. As a result, I began to understand what my parents were experiencing as their first child was leaving their family to start a new one. By apologizing, the two of us removed the tension that could easily have carried on to the wedding day and for years afterwards. Rather than becoming enemies, we shared one of the most meaningful moments of my life. Had I chosen the darker path, I am certain that my relationship with God and others would have suffered. Our actions, both positive and negative, have far-reaching consequences beyond what we might imagine.

If we take the time to sit down with those we've offended and with those who have offended us, we will be amazed at how many enemies become friends.

ATTAINING PERFECT HUMILITY
BY I. M. PROUD

Many times, conflict results from arrogance. We think or feel we deserve better treatment, or we're convinced that we have it all together, while others do not. Yet the Bible declares that we are to walk humbly before God and with others. We are all interconnected, which reminds us of our need for each other. The apostle Paul challenges the Romans to think differently, bathing his words with humility:

> For by the grace given me I say to every one of you: Do not think of yourself more highly than you ought, but rather think of yourself with sober judgment, in accordance with the faith

God has distributed to each of you. For just as each of us has one body with many members, and these members do not all have the same function, so in Christ we, though many, form one body, and each member belongs to all the others.

Romans 12:3 – 5

When we change our perspective and live with humility by acknowledging our need for God and others, everything changes. Acknowledging that we have needs implies that we need others to help meet those needs. As we look around with a humble perspective, we begin to discover that everyone has something unique about them and therefore has the capacity to make a unique contribution to our lives.

When people are in desperate need, suddenly whatever anger and bitterness they may have been struggling with disappears. Need seems to trump anger. For example, have you ever seen the loss of a family member bring people who had been estranged back together? If only there had been humility and a willingness by someone to say, "I don't care if I'm admitting defeat — I will humble myself and take the initiative to make things right because I need you in my life."

Too often we live life as though we have it all together, even while everyone else knows that we don't. Our weaknesses and imperfections are more obvious than we like to admit. We need to simply walk in humility, acknowledge that we're human and that we're prone to failure and to hurt and be hurt, but also that we are humble enough to do what it takes to make things right. We need to love more — even when we don't want to do so.

Love can so often float just beyond our reach as an abstract idea, but Paul had the uncanny ability to move love into the practical realm. Paul reminds us that love remains sincere, good, devoted, honoring, zealous, joyful, patient, faithful, generous, and hospitable (see Romans 12:9 – 13; 1 Corinthians 13). Love is a valuable commodity, worth more than the finest gold. Love is rare and precious, yet love is an act, a choice we can make.

Paul continues his thoughts on healthy relationships:

> Bless those who persecute you; bless and do not curse. Rejoice with those who rejoice; mourn with those who mourn. Live in harmony with one another. Do not be proud, but be willing to associate with people of low position. Do not think you are superior.
>
> Do not repay anyone evil for evil. Be careful to do what is right in the eyes of everyone. If it is possible, as far as it depends on you, live at peace with everyone. Do not take revenge, my dear friends, but leave room for God's wrath, for it is written: "It is mine to avenge; I will repay," says the Lord. On the contrary:
>
> > "If your enemy is hungry, feed him;
> > if he is thirsty, give him something to drink.
> > In doing this, you will heap burning coals on his head."
>
> Do not be overcome by evil, but overcome evil with good.
>
> **Romans 12:14 –21**

The truth of the matter is, following Christ actually creates conflict. A family member or a friend insists we join him or her in some nefarious activity, yet out of faithfulness to Christ we refuse. In the midst of genuine relationships with people, we will discover areas in which we disagree. For some, their relationship with Christ has led to persecution, imprisonment, or even the deaths of those closest to them. Yet in every case, we are to love and to keep on loving.

Blessing those who persecute us and refusing to repay evil for evil seems so counterintuitive, yet if Jesus could befriend Judas, the one who was to betray him, this is the least we can do. Even Solomon, the wisest person ever to have lived, implores us to live in a way that is counter to the pressures of the world when he writes, "When the LORD takes pleasure in anyone's way, he causes their enemies to make peace with them" (Proverbs 16:7).

Daily we face the opportunity to create conflict, prolong conflict, or end conflict. Too often we allow the actions of others to control us. We treat others in the same shoddy way they treated us — unless we resolve in our minds, "No matter what happens to me, I'm going to bless those who persecute me. I'm going to love those who hurt me. I'm going to do everything in my power, as far is it depends on me, to live at peace with everyone."

We should begin plotting sweet revenge — a different kind of revenge, a type of revenge whereby, rather than plotting vengeance, we actually look to serve and love our enemies. We need to move to the place where we look first to meet the needs of those with whom we fight.

If you've been in the position where you're the jerk of the story and somebody treats you kindly, that's the exact opposite of what you want, isn't it? When you're a jerk to someone, it's usually because you want them to be a jerk back. We want a fight, a rumble, so we can blame the other person for everything that has happened.

Kindness disarms our enemies. Remember, Paul reminded us that doing kind actions is like throwing burning coals on the heads of those who hate us (see Romans 12:20). Our kindness brings shame to those who hate us! Before we get too excited, however, we should realize that many times our kindness can turn an enemy into a friend.

How many times have our relationships ended up embroiled in conflict, only to be solved the moment we sat down to talk about it? We end up having fights in our minds with people before we sit down with them. We assume that things are much worse than they really are and that people have evil intentions, but those assumptions are usually just the result of a misunderstanding. Jesus, knowing that we lean toward pride and conflict, guides us toward lives filled with peace.

FIELD NOTES

In the early days of the multiethnic and economically diverse church I planted in Little Rock, Arkansas, we resurrected an old song that has particularly poignant meaning, singing the lyrics to envision our intended future:

We are one in the Spirit, we are one in the Lord,
We are one in the Spirit, we are one in the Lord.
And we pray that all unity will one day be restored:
And they'll know we are Christians by our love, by our love,
Yes, they'll know we are Christians by our love.

However, it didn't take long for us to realize that prayer alone will not restore unity to individuals who have entered into relational conflict. This is especially true when the people involved have built relationships across ethnic, cultural, or ideological divides.

As Eric explains in this chapter, forging or restoring relational unity with others who are different from you requires intentional effort driven by a passion to be at peace with all persons for the sake of the gospel. Along with prayer, then, success in this area will require a patient spirit and a persistent heart. At points, you will be forced to recognize that your way is only **one way** and not necessarily **the way** to understand another person or perspective. And this will further require of you humility, something in which we are not easily prone to walk.

Yes, in extending the love of God to others of different ethnic or economic backgrounds, there is a strong chance you will offend them along the way — and you may not know how to resolve the tension. When this happens, it will be difficult not to take things personally.

Our natural tendency is to grow hard-hearted toward those who push back. Or we will go to the opposite extreme and become compliant in order to avoid conflict and win their approval. Since neither response is appropriate or Christlike, we must learn to remain tenderhearted and gracious, even when sharing hard truths with others.

Therefore, be prepared to extend grace and mercy to all who offend you, knowing that wounded people react in wounding ways. Many are driven by deep-seated insecurities, sensitivities, and loyalties of which they are, for the most part, largely unaware. Consequently, they live in a state of self-deception and in bondage to the hurts or regrets of their past. Mix in diverse social or cultural perspectives, and the resulting conflicts can get quite complicated. On the other hand, these types of relationships — when patiently developed — can be like mortar to the bricks, forming a sturdy foundation of trust and authenticity between people of different back-grounds. The fact is that a single act of forgiveness to someone of another culture who has offended you will manifest the power of Christ to break dividing walls before all who witness it.

Keep in mind, too, that our spiritual enemy seeks to exploit our every insecurity in order to create misunderstanding, destroy trust, and under-mine the credibility of the gospel and of the church by causing division (Ephesians 6:12). You must be determined, however, not to let him win.

Yet even when we do all we can in such situations to live at peace with others (Romans 12:18), our efforts are not always rewarded. Sadly, someone will not retract a false accusation. Someone will not forgive you. And someone will leave the church in frustration. Yet, persecution is an unavoidable consequence for those who would be peacemakers and thus identified with Jesus (Matthew 5:9–12).

Perhaps there is no greater discouragement than being involved in a relational conflict with those you are sincerely seeking to love in the name of Christ. Nevertheless, do not lose heart in the midst of such times.

Rather, seek to prove that God is real through the power of love by being "completely humble and gentle; be patient, bearing with one another in love. Make every effort to keep the unity of the Spirit through the bond of peace" (Ephesians 4:2–3).

This is how to overcome uncivil war.

Indeed, this is how they'll know we are Christians — by our love.

Dr. Mark DeYmaz

Mark is founding pastor and directional leader of the Mosaic Church of Central Arkansas (*www .mosaicchurch.net*), a multiethnic and economically diverse church where men and women from more than thirty nations worship God together as one. He is the author of *Ethnic Blends* and a cofounder of Mosaix (*www.mosaix.info*), a relational network dedicated to inspiring unity and diversity in the local church throughout North America and beyond.

Chapter 6

WHITE MEN CAN JUMP (JUST NOT AS HIGH)

Seeing Past Stereotypes

"God is worthy! Hallelujah! He is worthy! Hallelujah!"

Those of us in his vicinity tried not to stare, although he appeared to want the attention. "He sure picked an interesting place to perform," I thought. We were in the terminal at Los Angeles International Airport, waiting for our direct flight from LAX to JFK in New York City.

At first his song had seemed unintelligible. After much straining, I could begin to understand the lyrics he was singing through his thick accent. His black shoes, slacks, and button-down shirt matched his black hair and mustache. The black hair on his arms covered his dark brown skin. He continued bellowing his tune for all to hear. He was alone, it seemed, yet why was he singing? He continued to pace back and forth as his song continued.

The date was September 19, 2001.

Eight days prior, the world had changed. As the next several days came and went, the story began to unfold. Hijackers. Terrorists. Osama bin Laden. Taliban. Heroes. Todd Beamer. New York City firefighters.

Everything was a blur during the course of those first few hours on September 11 and the following days, yet somewhere in the middle of it all, it hit me: Debbie, Caleb (two years old at the time), and I were flying into New York City to see friends and to speak at a youth conference the next week. Surely it would be canceled. I called the youth pastor to confirm my suspicions, but he told me that the students and the people in their church needed this retreat more than ever. Some people from his church had friends who had offices in the World Trade Center towers and who were still missing. He felt it would be good to have an outsider's perspective of hope and trust in God in the midst of such devastation.

In addition to the natural numbness I had been feeling, I now felt fear. I was expected to fly just days after the airports were allowed to reopen. I was flying at about the same time of day, on one of the same airlines, and between the same airports. Surely the youth group would understand if we could not come. "If it were just me, of course I would come" (I said to myself, hoping that it was true), but since Debbie and my two-year-old son were planning to travel with me — it was the perfect situation: Debbie and Caleb would be the reason for my withdrawal, not my own fear.

Just as I had hoped, Debbie did not want to go. She hated flying (an attitude that predated 9/11), but she did feel we should pray and seek advice before deciding. After a couple of days of vacillating, we decided that we wanted to be a part of helping people who were hurting. We began to feel that this was an opportunity God was placing before us and that he wanted us to respond in a spirit of trust and obedience.

Of course, we created an escape clause. I agreed with Debbie that if she did not feel comfortable flying to New York at any time before the trip, we would not hesitate to cancel the flight.

So then, up to this point in the days preceding the trip, all was proceeding smoothly. Once the Pavarotti wannabe chose to sing his own version of "This Is the Day," things began to unravel for us.

Just as the terminal singer concluded his song so he could get in line with his friend, we noticed that the two men in front of us also had dark brown skin and jet-black hair. Upon closer inspection, I could hear them speaking a foreign language, which I assumed was Arabic. Worse yet, they seemed to be big fans of cellophane. Both of their suitcases were wrapped tightly with sticky plastic wrap. How could the airport security check for bombs? Wasn't all of the luggage going to be opened and screened? We had arrived almost four hours ahead of our flight time because of the supposedly intense security. We watched as the woman at the gate checked in their bags and placed them on the conveyer belt. They were headed straight to the plane.

Debbie turned to me. "Didn't those guys with the plastic-wrapped luggage look like terrorists? Did you hear the song that guy was singing? These guys are plotting something!"

One of the advantages of marrying a woman who is prone to worry is that I get to be the courageous one. As she articulates what I am thinking, I have the chance to articulate the opposite. I become the more positive voice, even when I feel the same way she does. (And most of the time I do. Worrying seems to be in my genes — I have an aunt who once dialed 911 and hung up so that if she needed help while her husband was out of town she could just hit redial for a faster means of dialing. When I was a child, I wet my pants playing goalie in my first year of soccer, because the entire field of five-year-olds started running toward me all at once. When I was ten, my doctor had me on a bland diet to alleviate the ulcers I was developing while playing baseball — as a pitcher, I was afraid of hitting the batter with the ball.)

Somehow my verbal assurances that she was just being hypersensitive and that they were probably on a different flight backfired. Not only were these guys waiting to board our flight; another olive-skinned man was already in the waiting area when we arrived. The men did not sit together as they waited at the terminal — a strange thing, since we had seen two of them talking with each other in the baggage line earlier. Debbie was sure that the men were exchanging glances with each other over the tops of their newspapers and magazines. As one man seemed to wink at another, Debbie found her breaking point. She was still willing to fly to New York, but she did not want to go on this particular flight. She approached the woman at the counter to ask if there was an opportunity to transfer to the next flight.

"I'm sorry, ma'am, but your luggage is already on board this flight. We do not have time to remove your luggage. You will need to fly on this flight. We cannot allow you to switch."

I tried to persuade Debbie that all would be OK, in spite of the woman's response. I tried to point out once again that these four men were probably not the people she thought they were. For a time she seemed to have discovered enough peace to get on this flight.

She acknowledged to me that she was already afraid and that this experience was just accentuating her inner feelings.

As we boarded the plane, we noticed a disturbing scenario. The guy who had been singing was sweating profusely while wringing his hands and asking one of the flight attendants questions such as, "Can I move to the front of the plane? How many gallons of gas does this plane hold? Do we have enough gas in case we can't land immediately in New York?"

When we finally reached our row, which happened to be filled with mujahideen,[1] Debbie continued moving toward the back. She was carrying Caleb in her arms, and she had her own set of questions for another flight attendant. Unfortunately, this flight attendant seemed to be more upset by the current state of events than Debbie. As Debbie asked to be allowed to get off the plane and book a later flight, tears began to slide down her cheeks. The flight attendant empathized with Debbie; she was scared too. Debbie was now more afraid than ever. She came back to me to invoke our escape clause. She was not going to fly on this plane. The flight attendant from the front of the plane approached us as we began gathering up our things. "I'm sorry, but you cannot leave this flight. Your luggage must travel with you. Please be seated so we can begin our flight."

Now we were being held hostage by American Airlines employees wearing name tags and polyester dress suits. Terrified that the men seated in our row knew enough English to have understood our conversation, I bounced back and forth between looking straight ahead and looking at Debbie. I did not want to make eye contact with these guys, fearing that my family and I would be their first victims.

Within a few minutes, the flight attendant returned and asked us to gather our things. We were now going to be allowed to exit the plane — apparently we were scaring the other passengers.

STEREOTYPES

If we are honest with ourselves, we all have to admit that at times we find ourselves stereotyping others. We allow the words of others, bad experiences from our past, news reports, and even our fears to be projected onto others so that we form prejudicial judgments against others. None of us like to be seen in light of a stereotype, but we do not seem to hesitate to do the same to others. Think of the last time you made a decision or chose a course of action based on a stereotype of another person. It's quite likely that you won't have to remember back too far into your past.

After getting off that particular flight at LAX, we got on the next flight. This flight also had men and women from Arab heritage, yet without the singing and the cellophane, we were able to ride with relative peace (as much peace as possible on a plane in that time in history). Of course, the other plane had been filled not with terrorists but with scared men, just like us. We had allowed the images of Al Qaeda operatives to move our minds to lump into their category all one billion Muslims and anyone with a hint of Middle Eastern heritage. Too often we assume the worst in others, limiting the possibilities of others based on their appearance. I'm thankful that Caleb is too young to remember this lapse in our lives, because so often our children and those we influence absorb and live out the same stereotypes we hold.

Stereotypes exist because we do not form friendships with others who differ from us. We assume everyone from an entire race of people has the same character or idiosyncrasies. As a result, taxi drivers in New York or police officers in certain parts of the country racially profile others, targeting them on the basis of their race. Some taxi drivers don't stop for those with dark skin, while some police officers look for those with dark skin to stop.

One night at dinner with some of the leaders at our church, we began talking about racial profiling. One man shared about how a police officer slowly followed him as he walked with his friends when he was a teenager. After following them for quite a while, the police officer cautioned the white kids to be careful about hanging out with a "troublemaker." The "troublemaker" had never gotten into trouble with the law; he just happened to be Hispanic. Another leader spoke of the time the police pulled him over because he was a Latino driving a nice car. Apparently, he matched the description of a carjacking suspect. The officer let him go with a warning to "watch your speed," even though he hadn't been speeding. (This is the same friend of mine who gets "randomly" searched at airports every time he sports a goatee — which doesn't happen when he is clean-shaven.)

One of the others told of the massacre of Chinese immigrants in Los Angeles about one hundred years ago, a story I knew little about. In October 24, 1871, after a Caucasian man had been accidentally shot and killed, many of the white residents blamed the Chinese immigrants, even though no one ever found the killer. Hundreds of Caucasians flooded into Chinatown, ransacking homes, robbing people, killing about twenty boys and men, and then hanging their bodies for all to see. Another friend at the table had family members who had experienced the Japanese internment camp during World War II. We talked about how Asian bias and stereotypes seem to continue today in less violent yet subtler ways and how Hollywood seems to forget that Asians even exist. NBC's *Suddenly Susan*, which took place in San Francisco, a city populated with many Asian-Americans, did not include one Asian in its cast. *Joan of Arcadia*, which took place in Arcadia High School, included some very interesting characters such as Joan, who wrestled with her relationship with God, and her brother Kevin, who faced the challenge of paralysis after being hit by a drunk driver. However, *Joan of Arcadia* was strikingly devoid of Asian characters. The Arcadia High School I know in the LA area is in a predominantly Asian area, and about two-thirds of the students are Asian. The only times Asians seem to be on television or in films is when they are beating up someone with their martial arts moves.

Everyone seemed to keep sharing more and more stories of how "the man" had let them or their people down. It was one of those moments when everyone is trying to share a story more impressive than the previous one — you know, the "Oh yeah? Well, one time . . ." kind of storytelling that progressed around the table. I kept thinking to myself, "It's almost my turn. I've got to think of a good one. I'm the youngest one here, and I've got to fit in." As the only Caucasian guy at the table, I had a problem, though. I look like "the man." The system had never betrayed me. When I got pulled over by the police, it was because I was actually speeding. After my mind came back with examples from working in East LA or teaching in downtown Los Angeles, I decided to simply ask questions. This was my chance to learn from friends who had a different experience in their interactions with others in this world. The stories were never bitter, just honest, as they casually shared about their experiences of being victims of a stereotype.

In extreme instances, stereotyping can have deadly results. Jean Charles de Menezes, a Brazilian electrician, had just boarded a train at the Stockwell tube station in London when he was shot several times in the head and killed by British police because they suspected, by his appearance, that he was a suicide bomber. He supposedly ran from the plainclothes officers; I would run too if strangers were running at me, pointing guns in my direction. Just perusing news stories from the last few years, I have seen reports of a black man who decided to kill the next white woman he saw, white kids who killed a young black man with an ax because of his ethnicity, a burning cross in a front yard meant to scare a black family in North Carolina, and men wearing KKK hoods and sheets in an attempt to force out Hispanics in Ohio.

Most of us do not act out violently against others based on their ethnicity, but what are we doing to ensure that this type of injustice stops? When we decide not to help solve the problem, we allow the momentum to continue toward injustice. In our family, we have a slogan: "Don't complain about anything you aren't willing to do anything about." This should be true in every area of our lives, not just when it comes to doing the dishes or experiencing conflict with a family member.

When we fail to befriend those who are not like us, we miss out. Remaining cocooned in our own little world with no desire to venture outside keeps us from experiencing many remarkable conversations, foods, scents, and dances. More important, fear keeps us from discovering many remarkable friendships. As followers of Christ, we need to actively befriend anyone God brings into our lives. Our world is becoming more and more diverse, so much so that to remain homogenous in our churches and in our friendships actually takes effort. Instead, we need to be more intentional to live out the second part of the Great Commandment — to love our neighbor — even those who look different from us. The nations are now living all around us, and not just in our largest cities. God has moved people from around the world into our lives so that we may show Christ's love. What about the people in India who have never heard about Jesus? Some of them just moved in down the street.

Sadly, as a religion, Christianity has not fared well when it comes to race relations. Those who claimed to follow Christ have attacked, oppressed, and killed Arabs during the Crusades, Jews during the Spanish Inquisition, Africans during the slave trade — and on and on we could go. Within recent memory, white "Christians" who were part of the Ku Klux Klan actively sought to segregate, intimidate, and even kill blacks because of their skin color. We may try to navigate the world with more political correctness, but what are we doing to show the world that we represent God's love for all people?

Political correctness attempts to change the words we say, but it fails to change the way we feel. We act as though everything is OK on the surface, but are things really different?

Too often we seem to "yell" at those in our nation who have different values, while failing to realize that we're not upset about the right things. The world hears what we oppose very clearly; therefore, we need to begin voicing whom we support that much more.

"REFUGEES" FROM NEW ORLEANS

In 2005 thousands of men, women, and children were trapped by the floodwaters caused by Hurricane Katrina. With tears in their eyes as they stood in front of the many thousands of "refugees," reporters shouted out what was happening. This was not some horrible tragedy befalling the people of Bangladesh or Pakistan. We were watching the city of New Orleans fight to survive. The "Big Easy" had become a big pool of toxic soup, forcing thousands upon thousands from their homes. As some were being rescued from their attics and others were waiting for food and water at the Superdome, stories of looting and raping — and even stories about "pirates" stealing boats — flooded the airwaves. With images of thousands of seemingly helpless people projected on our TV screens, we felt powerless to help. How could we let Americans — or anyone, for that matter — endure so much? How could we allow so many days to pass without help from the government? How could we not have been better prepared for this type of catastrophe? What can we do to help even now?

Like most churches, at Mosaic we began spreading the word about ways to get involved in serving those who had been displaced by the devastation of Hurricane Katrina. People gave thousands of dollars, and we mobilized about twenty people to go to Houston for ten days. Raising their own support and taking time off from work and school, these women and men went to serve at the Astrodome and the Reliant Center just days after the buses had arrived. Our team members ranged in age from their early twenties to mid-forties, and our team included some of our interns who had moved from the Midwest and South to serve in Los Angeles, as well as several people who had grown up in Southern California. Thanks to the generosity of several churches in the Houston area, team members found housing and transportation — and the opportunity to get involved directly with those seeking refuge after losing their homes. The group worked tirelessly in multiple ways, transporting families to the airport, bus station, and apartments; unloading supplies donated from people and organizations across the country; playing with the children; and so on.

Our group included Anglos, Asian-Americans, and one African-American named Dawn. Something strange began to happen to the team as the week transpired. As most of the group found open access throughout the work areas, Dawn kept running into barriers. The workers from the Red Cross and from FEMA would order Dawn to return to the Astrodome rather than allowing her to continue walking with the rest of her team. They were assuming that Dawn, being African-American, needed help, rather than seeing her as someone who had come to give help. As the week continued, other workers kept on treating Dawn as a second-class citizen. The rest of the team from our church became more and more frustrated by the way Dawn was being treated, as well as by the way they sensed that government workers were treating the evacuees.

After spending several hours playing with children whose parents were out searching for new places to live, Dawn was approached by one of the workers and rebuked for spending time with these kids. (The worker didn't reprimand the white woman from our team who was playing with the kids as well.) As the conversation continued, the worker blurted out that she feared for the children's safety. She thought Dawn was befriending these children in order to kidnap them.

Hurricane Katrina rather strikingly revealed the racial tension in our nation that had been covered by a thin veil of political correctness. Many outspoken African-Americans complained that the response had been slow because those needing help were black. Even the use of the term "refugee" seemed to expose that white America had been thinking of the inner city as a place filled with foreigners who needed help. The media showed pictures of African-Americans who were "looting," while showing pictures of Caucasian people in New Orleans who were "finding food."

Even though the response from predominantly white states in our country seemed to be overwhelmingly positive, there still seemed to be a mentality of "us" and "them." Dawn experienced this firsthand in Houston. Almost all of the people who needed help appeared to be black Americans; almost all of the people providing help appeared to be white Americans. This imagery seemed to perpetuate the idea that black people need white people. Dawn did not fit that stereotype. As a result, people struggled to see her in any other capacity. Dawn was a black person serving as part of a multiethnic team helping those in need. She did not fit the box in which others wanted to place her.

Too often the church falls into a dangerous mind-set. We like to help people, just as long as they don't get too close. We may partner with churches of different ethnicities, yet we work together for a short time and from a distance. For example, members of a predominately Anglo church may feel good about themselves when they go into an inner-city neighborhood that is predominantly African-American, or an African-American church may take a mission trip into Mexico, but are we reaching out to those who are different from us who live or work beside us?

And what about those around us who do not need our help? Are we getting to know those people who live in our community and whom we encounter at work — no matter how different they may be from us? We need to move from meetings that just *talk* about racial reconciliation and actually create communities that show the world we *are* reconciled.

GLIMPSE OF HEAVEN

"The great philosopher Rodney King once asked, 'Can't we all get along? Can't we all just get along?' We have proven throughout history that the answer to his question is 'No!' Throughout history, we have discovered we cannot get along with each other. Ironically, we seem to despise those who look just like us, not just those who do not."

Erwin McManus, the lead pastor at Mosaic, was sharing these words with a predominantly white church in Orange County. The church had invited Erwin because they were very interested in becoming a diverse community, and they wanted to start a service for Latinos or Filipinos.

At that time, I had been volunteering at Mosaic for several months before being asked to serve in the youth ministry. I was facing some challenges as a white youth pastor of a primarily Latino youth group in East Los Angeles. In fact, Erwin found himself having to defend my appointment when one Latino leader had questioned why he would choose a white guy for this position. In the midst of this transition, Erwin had invited me to join him as he spoke at this rather affluent church about reaching out to other ethnicities. I was listening attentively, hoping to learn anything that might help me in my new role.

As Erwin continued his talk that day, he pointed out the bitter and homicidal feuds between the Hutus and Tutsis in Rwanda, the Bosnians and Serbs in the Baltics, and the Protestants and Catholics in Ireland. Though we may not be able to discern the differences, those involved are very aware of those they hate with a murderous passion.

When Erwin asked all those in attendance who had coworkers or neighbors from different ethnic backgrounds to raise their hands, almost everyone did so. However, when asked how many of these coworkers or neighbors had ever been invited over for dinner, hands went down. The atmosphere in the room grew awkward as Erwin went on to say, "If you want to become a diverse church, you need to have friends from diverse backgrounds. Many of us *say* we want diversity — but only if our children don't marry their children."

These well-meaning men and women wanted some tips for starting a service either for Latinos or for Filipinos. They were OK with this type of diversity. I even think they were willing to hear about racial reconciliation. The cold response from the crowd made me think that many people there were not quite ready to live out a life that is reconciled to others, but I must be careful — I could be stereotyping them.

As human beings, we are extremely complex. We punch our younger brothers, but we defend them when they are attacked by others. We act as though we are being protective, but in reality maybe we simply want to maintain our privileges as the only ones allowed to beat them up. We huddle up in homogenous churches, yet we fight insatiably in those churches. In essence, we are all out for ourselves. If banding together with those who look like us is more beneficial, then we do so; if hating those who look just like us advances our own selfish cause, then so be it. I think we can all admit it: people are selfish. Without God's help we will fight any who stand in our way within our community and especially those outside of it.

The early church miraculously moved toward inclusion in its early days. During Pentecost, the disciples experienced a linguistic miracle: they spoke in the languages of those who had come to Jerusalem for the holiday. Women and men from Libya, Rome, Egypt, Crete, Cappadocia, Mesopotamia, and "every nation under heaven" (Acts 2:5) were transformed by God. As a result, the church was born in diversity. Throughout history, diversity has continued in the universal church, but for the vast majority of local churches, diversity disappeared somewhere along the way. God's passion has always been for the nations, as evidenced throughout the Scriptures from Genesis to Revelation — from the time God chose Abraham in order to bless "all peoples on earth" (Genesis 12:3) to the song that acknowledges that Christ's blood "purchased for God members of every tribe and language and people and nation" (Revelation 5:9). In a time in history when "the nations" live together in the same cities, most of our churches remain homogenous. More often than not, it is not language that keeps us from each other; it is our unwillingness to make the necessary sacrifices to reach and empower the "nations" within our churches.

Recent solutions for ethnic tension do not go far enough. Tolerance and racial reconciliation were steps in the right direction, but they didn't get us to where we should be. We end up acknowledging that another group has value, but we act as though their value is best appreciated from a distance.

Tolerance has often been touted as a great accomplishment. Leaders in politics, education, athletics, and business promote equality and integration, yet in practice we remain isolated from each other. To be sure, tolerance remains better than animosity, but it's still not as good as genuine concern, care, and affection. None of us truly long to be tolerated; we all long to be loved. Tolerance allows us to survive; love allows us to thrive. As a global community, we need to break through tolerance and embrace love. When we become tired of tolerating others, we should try loving them.

An alternative option for some has been to become "colorblind," but this strategy falls short since color blindness ignores an important part of a person's identity. We should see beyond someone's color so that we get to know the person; but to truly get to know a person, we need to find out what being black, brown, beige, or white is like. Our ethnic background shapes us. At the same time, we are so much more complex than our appearance. Our families, our socioeconomic status, our personality, our strengths, our talents, our passions, and our experiences all make us unique.

I am fortunate to work with an amazing group of people at Mosaic. We have two female leaders on our team named Dana — one is Dana Evans and the other Dana Elliott. Dana Evans is Anglo, and Dana Elliott is African-American. In addition to having offices next to each other, these two Danas are also roommates. You can imagine how many times people have confused one of them as the other one. One day I mentioned to Caleb, who was six years old at the time, that Dana was coming over to see him and his sister. My kids love both Danas. Caleb looked at me with a curious expression as he asked, "Which Dana — the brown one or the peach one?" Six-year-old boys are not very politically correct, but it would have been silly for him to overlook their skin tone as a distinguishing characteristic. What was beautiful for me in that moment was that for Caleb the difference between the two wasn't as stark as black and white; he saw them as different shades of brown.

In heaven, racial boundaries will not exist. So why are boundaries so prevalent on earth? At one of our recent Sunday gatherings, a non-Christian who was visiting noticed the diverse crowd and said, "If I believed in heaven, it would look like this." If we aren't willing to diversify in order to connect to God's heart, then we should be willing to diversify to show God's heart to those in our lives who do not yet follow Christ. Our world is much more diverse. My daughter, Trevi, has a better chance of growing up to marry a Chen or a Ramirez than to marry a Smith or a Jones.

Furthermore, people are becoming more diverse themselves. Rather than representing just a mixture of European cultures,

Americans are a blend of Latino, African, Asian, Middle Eastern, and European — sometimes all in one person. The path to diversity begins with the mission of Christ. When we choose to reach out and love everyone around us, we will experience a glimpse of heaven on earth.

FIELD NOTES

One of the greatest challenges each one of us faces is how to transform an issue from black-and-white into flesh and blood.

Black-and-white is always easier. Simpler. Safer.

Love requires us to move beyond snap judgments to know, to embrace, to understand — even when we ourselves don't feel understood. Love requires that we clasp humanity.

In order to become part of the solution to all the isms that plague our society — racism, sexism, ageism, as well as countless others — we must be intentional about having people in our lives who are different from us. People who challenge what we believe and why we believe it. People who expand our hearts so they're bigger than our heads. People who help us see another perspective we'd never develop on our own. People who turn mere black-and-white issues into flesh and blood. That means getting to know different kinds of people from different ethnicities, socio-economic backgrounds, and belief systems.

Why is this so crucial? Because when you get to know a someone rather than just read about a something in the newspaper, a subtle but significant change happens. We find that we're no longer talking about issues; we're talking about people we have come to know and love. The conclusions we draw from encountering the face of humanity transform us. It may or may not change our conclusions, but it will always change our tone — filling us with grace, hope, and gentleness that we would not have otherwise. And in the process, we can't help but look a little bit more like Jesus.

Margaret Feinberg

Margaret (*www.margaretfeinberg.com*) is a popular speaker and the author of *Scouting the Divine*, *The Organic God*, and dozens of other books and Bible studies. Follow her on Twitter (mafeinberg) or become her friend on Facebook.

Chapter 7

THE UNTOUCHABLES

Learning to See Those We Overlook

Some of my friends had chosen to dig through a Dumpster behind Pizza Hut for lunch. Dumpster-diving had not interested me that day. I might have been poor, but I liked to retain a certain level of cleanliness. Germs and I had never really gotten along. Instead, I had chosen to walk to the Salvation Army. Sure, their meals were cold too, but at least they weren't hard to find. Options were limited, living on the streets.

The sun was beating down on me. I was amazed at how hot the day could be after the evening had been so cold. I was beginning to regret my choice of attire. Corduroys and a long-sleeve shirt would definitely make the nights easier to take, but they were beginning to ruin my days.

A few other homeless men were already waiting for the daily food rationing. At twenty-one years of age, I was by far the youngest. Several of these men seemed to have been alive forever, for they barely looked alive now. Years on the street had cut deep lines into their faces. The skin on their hands and arms was rough and cracked, as though they had experienced years of labor, yet more than likely the calluses were the result of years in the elements. I stood quietly at the end of the line, waiting for the meal distribution to begin.

The man right in front of me had paint all over his jacket and shoes. Curious, I asked him what had happened. He explained that he had been getting paid to paint walls at a church building down the way.

Before I could continue the conversation, a man named Rex lined up behind me. (I knew his name was Rex because he had written "REX" on his hand.) He offered me a cigarette and then began telling us how he had been kicked out of the VA hospital because of his injuries. I had never heard of someone who was kicked out of a hospital because of their injuries until Rex explained: an ant had crawled into his ear, and when he tried to kill the ant with a stick, he punctured his eardrum. Before Rex could share more of the nasty details, the Salvation Army lieutenants or generals — whatever you call those who serve the food there — opened the door by the dining area. It was time to eat.

Cold chicken tenders, cheese poofs (aka fake Cheetos), and a pint of milk hit the spot. The cardboard box filled with milk proved to be somewhat problematic at first. I couldn't get that sucker to open right. I pulled at the V section, but the seal never opened. I had to poke a hole through the seal with my dirty fingers to pull away the opening. I hate it when that happens!

Just before heading out for my next item to scavenge, I noticed that the fellow with paint splattered all over him seemed to be admiring my shoes. The rest of my outfit may have provoked laughter earlier in the day as I walked past a group of teenagers, but these shoes were now provoking interest. I loved my shoes. They were snazzy. The gray meshy material covered with a darker gray design looked good. Best of all, they *felt* good. I needed those comfortable shoes for my adventures on the streets. Deep inside somewhere, I knew I should talk with him again. It was deep inside, near my heart — a place called my conscience, I think.

"How long have you been on the streets?" I asked.

"A few years. Ever since my mom died." He looked like a stranger to the indoors. I guessed he may have been in his forties. Gray hairs intermingled with his black hairs. His hair was fluffy on one side and flat on the other. It was as though he had a comb for his Afro for only half the necessary grooming time, or as though he had been getting ready in front of a mirror that showed only half his face. I had noticed a few teeth missing and only nine and a half fingers. I discovered that his name was Leonard.

"Want to try on these shoes?" I had hesitated to offer at first, but the more I stood there watching him inhale his cheese poofs as though they were the greatest source of nourishment known to mankind, the more certain I had become.

"No. I was just noticing them and wondering where to get me some like that. I know how important good walking shoes are." He began licking the cheese poof residue off the four and a half fingers of his left hand.

"Let's just see if they fit. They're too big for me." I sat down to undo the Velcro on my snazzy gray shoes. He shrugged his shoulders and slipped off his beat-up brown shoes. They looked like penny loafers without the pennies.

As proud as I had been to wear those gray shoes, I was even more proud to see him wearing them. It was as though they were the greatest Christmas present he'd ever received. After fastening them, he jumped up and down, testing their quite excellent bounce. They had enough cushion to make you think you were walking with shock absorbers. I started walking away with a smile on my face.

"Hey! How long have you been on the streets?" I could tell he was trying to continue the conversation as a way of thanking me.

"Oh," I said, turning around to see his not-so-toothy grin, "I became homeless yesterday afternoon, and I'll be back in my dorm tomorrow night. I'm taking part in a poverty simulation weekend with my school."

"Great! Have fun with that, and thanks for the shoes!"

SIMULATED POVERTY

During my class called "Poverty in Waco," we were required to attend a poverty simulation. Jimmy and Janet Dorrell lead Mission Waco, an organization committed to serving some of the poorest areas in Waco, Texas. (Waco is not a large place, but even in a city of one hundred thousand people located halfway between Dallas and Austin, there are plenty of people who have genuine needs.) The Dorrells live in an underprivileged neighborhood, lead a church for the homeless who hang out under a freeway interstate, serve the city's impoverished, and expose Baylor students, among others, to life on the streets. The experience opened my eyes to an entirely new world. As a result, I took my youth group and Debbie, who was then my girlfriend, to the next poverty simulation. I wanted them to catch a glimpse of what it looked like to actively serve those in need.

After welcoming us, the Dorrells shared the ground rules. "This weekend we are not going to simply talk about serving the homeless. You are going to *experience* homelessness. Choose two items from your suitcases to keep, excluding clothes. Everything else will be locked away for the entire weekend."

Panic ensued. The participants started asking, "Should I keep a toothbrush, my Bible, my sleeping bag, a pillow, my teddy bear? What should I keep?" Some began negotiating with each other. "I'll keep my glasses and toothbrush if you'll keep your sleeping bag and toothpaste so we can share." Sharing a toothbrush? Hey, desperate times called for desperate measures!

Since I had already experienced the weekend, I knew what to choose. I kept my sleeping bag and my comb I wanted to sleep good and look good. Debbie ended up choosing her purse and her sleeping bag. After being reprimanded for trying to keep her purse and reminded she could only have *two items*, she chose her toothbrush and sleeping bag. When a headache later began pounding in her temple, she began to despise "the game." When I bring up that weekend, she usually reminds me that she could have died without her Tylenol.

One of the kids in my youth group, Wesley, chose not to keep anything. As we discovered throughout the weekend, Wesley was excellent at living on the streets. He ended up making more money panhandling throughout the weekend than what he had to spend for the retreat. He was *too* good at being poor. After the simulation ended, we had to convince Wesley to go home to live in his house with his family rather than staying on the street for the rest of the week.

As I've gotten to know my wife over the years, I realize now why the poverty simulation was not a good experience for her. She is full of empathy and concern for others. She did not have to live as a homeless woman to see the world as those in poverty see it. She has a natural knack for loving people who are often overlooked. For me, on the other hand, the dirt under my fingernails, the growling stomach, the pointing, and the humiliation were necessary to help me see people I had never seen before. Walking in their raggedy brown dress shoes changed my life.

SEEING THE OBVIOUS

Growing up working as a carpenter and preparing for the revolution he was about to unleash, Jesus came across a unique moment in his life that would define his future and the path for all who would follow him throughout history. After fasting for forty days and overcoming a face-to-face encounter with Satan himself, Jesus was prepared for this unique moment. Jesus was about to preach his first sermon in Nazareth, where he had grown up.

The act of preaching is quite a scary prospect. I remember the questions that filled my mind before my first sermon. What if they laugh when I'm sharing something I intended to be serious? What if they cry when I really meant to be funny? What if no one responds at all? What if I forget what I'm supposed to say? What if I say something I didn't mean to say? Having heard many mistakes from pastors along the way, I was nervous. Thank goodness, my first message was shared before the Internet was created to pass along the many mistakes of those who were trying to preach about God but because of a slip of the tongue are now infamous. (I'm sure you've heard the audio of the guy who meant to say "pitched his tents"; if not, look online without any kids nearby.)

Speaking publicly in front of those who already know you is even scarier. Sure, they may seem to be more forgiving since, hopefully, they like you; but they also know you, and they will see you again after the preaching moment comes to an end. Any mistake made would be forever remembered and resurrected at the most inopportune moments. I preached my first sermon at the place where I was involved as a teenager, and it came during a youth-led service at Shady Oaks Baptist Church in Hurst, Texas. Originally, I was just supposed to share my testimony, but once our senior pastor, Dr. John W. Bobo, heard that I was interested in pursuing ministry in the future, what was originally going to be a two-minute story about how God had changed my life mutated to become a thirty-minute sermon. Seeing Sunday school teachers in the crowd who were familiar with my former extracurricular activities made me that much more self-conscious. I was so nervous I spoke extremely quickly. Without intending to do so, I finished in a record-breaking seven minutes. Sure, it was longer than the two-minute testimony would have been, but it was also quite underwhelming and embarrassing. I'm sure there were many who thought I should reconsider my pursuit of ministry in favor of any job that wouldn't require standing in front of others while talking.

Jesus' first sermon back home had worse results. He was almost killed by his neighbors and former Saturday school teachers. Had he allowed an inappropriate word to slip out of his mouth when he actually intended to say something else? Had he called his hearers out for secret sins that he made public? What on earth did Jesus say in his homecoming message?

Standing in front of those who knew Jesus and his family, Jesus proclaimed his purpose for living and, as we know now, his reason for dying. Jesus read from a scroll:

"The Spirit of the Lord is on me,
    because he has anointed me
    to proclaim good news to the poor.

He has sent me to proclaim freedom for the prisoners
   and recovery of sight for the blind,
   to set the oppressed free,
   to proclaim the year of the Lord's favor."

Luke 4:18 – 19, quoting from Isaiah 61:1 – 2; Isaiah 58:6

Rolling up the scroll, Jesus sat down. With everyone's eyes focused on him, Jesus continued his brief yet earth-shattering message: "Today this scripture is fulfilled in your hearing" (Luke 4:21). The response from the crowd: "Isn't that cute? That's Joseph's little boy all grown up" (my paraphrase of Luke 4:22).

Certainly by this time, many of Jesus' neighbors and friends had heard about some of his adventures and good deeds in the surrounding areas. They loved the idea that a prophet was rising up from their neighborhood. They were excited to be able to tell their friends, "I knew Jesus way before anyone else had even heard of him." They were also excited that they would soon be the recipients of God's special blessing. The miraculous works of God were about to begin!

The people in the crowd seemed to like the idea that Jesus was going to help the poor, the imprisoned, the sick, and the oppressed. We tend to appreciate when other people do good things for those in need. In some ways it helps us feel better about not being involved, knowing that at least *someone* is doing the hard work.

Knowing that they hadn't heard what he said but just liked the fact that he had said anything at all, Jesus continued to explain to them that this was no ordinary homecoming message:

> Jesus said to them, "Surely you will quote this proverb to me:
> 'Physician, heal yourself!' And you will tell me, 'Do here in your
> hometown what we have heard that you did in Capernaum.'

"Truly I tell you," he continued, "prophets are not accepted in their hometowns. I assure you that there were many widows in Israel in Elijah's time, when the sky was shut for three and a half years and there was a severe famine throughout the land. Yet Elijah was not sent to any of them, but to a widow in Zarephath in the region of Sidon. And there were many in Israel with leprosy in the time of Elisha the prophet, yet not one of them was cleansed — only Naaman the Syrian."

All the people in the synagogue were furious when they heard this. They got up, drove him out of the town, and took him to the brow of the hill on which the town was built, in order to throw him off the cliff. But he walked right through the crowd and went on his way.

Luke 4:23 – 30

In the midst of the crowd's enthusiasm, Jesus shared news that turned the crowd against him: all of those good things he just read about from the scroll would not happen in Nazareth, for the town's residents did not see Jesus as they should. He was more than just a carpenter. He was more than just Joseph's son. He was a prophet and a messenger of God, and — even more remarkable and hard for them to believe — he was God's Son. Jesus could not care for the poor or oppressed in his hometown because they didn't see him as capable of doing so. To them, Jesus was just a normal guy. Jesus was offering hope for people who needed help, but this help would not be forced. It was by invitation only — and his former friends and neighbors were not inviting him.

When Jesus shifted the focus of his efforts of blessing to those who were outside Nazareth and even used an example of God's blessing dirty Gentiles (Naaman the Syrian), rage replaced excitement. The people loved the idea of a special blessing for themselves but not for others. How could God not bestow a special blessing on them alone? After all, they were the people of Israel!

Bitter feelings soon gave way to angry actions. The crowd rose up, pointing fingers and yelling at Jesus, pushing, shoving, and moving him and everyone else out of the synagogue and away from the town. As frustrations boiled over, Jesus found himself on the edge of a cliff, on the edge of losing his life. With courage and resolve, Jesus escaped danger. This was not his day to die. With the power of God at his fingertips, he could have readily and decisively showed this crowd who he was. He could have proven to these former neighbors that he had power they never could have imagined was possible. With a wave of his hand he could have disappeared or summoned angry angels to surround the crowd or even brought in a flaming chariot into which he could have jumped to carry out his dramatic getaway. Instead, Jesus did something more spectacular: he walked through the angry mob and continued his journey. Jesus would not be stopped.

As a Gentile, I become excited by the very thing that enraged the people of Nazareth. I am glad God decided to expand his blessing from just those in Israel to include all peoples on earth. In reality, these Israelites had forgotten that even their blessing as God's people was to lead toward the blessing of all nations (see Genesis 12:1 – 3). God's blessing was not to be held hostage or hoarded but shared with others.

Before we are too hard on this crowd, we should be honest with our own response to Jesus' words. When I was growing up, I remember hearing that we were "the new children of God." We had replaced Israel as "the nation under God." I am referring not to those who choose to follow Christ (i.e., the church) but to the United States of America. I remember being taught that the United States of America was now "the nation blessed by God" to be "a blessing to the nations." For proof, all we had to do was look at the word "Jerusalem." Can you see the proof? Right there in the middle of the City of Zion are three important letters. Do you see them? Jer**usa**lem. The USA was the new Jerusalem. How would we feel if we were being told that God's blessing was no longer upon us but was upon Korea, El Salvador, Kenya, or China?

If I am truly honest, had I heard Jesus' first sermon when I was younger, I would have had a mixed reaction. The second part of Jesus' message would have inspired me. I am not from Nazareth, and I am not Jewish. Jesus' promise to bless the Gentiles means a blessing on me! To this, I say, "Bring it on!" However, the first part of the message would *not* have inspired me; it would have scared me or perhaps even angered me.

From the very beginning, Jesus set his sights on serving those on the margins of society — the poor, the disabled, the oppressed, the forgotten, the untouchables. That would not have interested me because I didn't see any of these as describing me. From a purely selfish perspective, it appears that Jesus' message and his ministry are not for me — a white guy who grew up in the suburbs and has never been blind or in jail. I may not have started a riot sitting in that room where Jesus spoke, but I certainly would have looked for someone else to follow. What kind of fool does Jesus think I am to ask me to pour out my life in service to people who are "less than me"? I want a leader who is committed to meeting *my* needs! I want to follow someone who is devoted to *me*! Who is Jesus to stand in front of me and invite me to lay down my life for others when I haven't even found happiness or joy in *my* life?

Since I have embraced a relationship with Jesus, I have come to realize that I'm more of an outcast than I realized. I need God more than I ever would have wanted to admit. At the same time, I have come to discover that when Jesus promised we would find our lives only as we lose our lives in serving others, he was telling the truth (see Matthew 10:39; Mark 10:42–45; John 12:24–26).

Jesus chose carefully the text he would read that day in his hometown of Nazareth. He could have chosen thousands of different verses that would have pointed out his greatness and his arrival as Savior. Instead, Jesus chose to point out God's heart for the "least of these" (Matthew 25:40). Since the world fails to care for those with the greatest need, Jesus would care, and he would call all who follow him to do the same.

RELEARNING AGAIN

Have you ever forgotten what you have already known? I love the phrase I've heard people use to describe intelligent people: "She has forgotten more than I will ever know." For me, I tend to have the same experiences over and over. It seems as though I really understand what God is teaching me, but then I forget again and need to relearn — or at least be reminded.

I think as followers of Christ we go through these cycles. There is so much more for us to learn, yet we need to retrace our previous steps. Throughout history, Christians have been at the forefront of caring for the marginalized and overlooked. A remnant of the church has always been present among the poor. In more recent memory, the Salvation Army, Sojourners, and World Impact, as well as many others, have not only called the church to get involved in the lives of the underprivileged; they have mobilized millions of people as well. Sadly, at the same time, many churches have moved away from poverty-stricken neighborhoods and especially out of the cities. Most of evangelical America tends to be hunkered down in the suburbs, just beyond the reach of the inner city.

Somewhere along the way, Christians in the Western world began to veer in one of two directions: some saw the gospel as being about compassion and social justice, yet their theology moved to the left; a more conservative approach maintained a high view of the Scriptures yet saw the gospel as moving a person toward personal conversion. One group met the physical and social needs of the person, while perhaps skimping on the spiritual, while the other group was all about the spiritual needs, yet it overlooked the obvious physical and social conditions.

I think both are right and both are wrong. We should seek to meet both the physical and the spiritual needs of a person, working to help the situation and the person change. During my college days, I knew this to be true while trying to reach people in a "transitional" neighborhood. I knew it to be true in Seattle while reaching out to a family with a mom who had twelve kids with four different dads, and I know it to be true in LA, serving among some of our families at Mosaic and in our city. Yet I tend to forget so very quickly too. I start getting busy doing good things and forget the great things to which I am called.

In Waco, I truly enjoyed serving as a youth pastor. It was quite a challenge to be part of an older Caucasian group located in more of an African-American and Latino neighborhood. The teens I began to befriend didn't fit in at the church. In addition to the obvious ethnic differences, these kids were from a different socioeconomic class than those who came to our weekly church services. One of the challenges we faced as a church was the frequent number of requests for money that came from people in the neighborhood. The policy was to refer these folks who needed assistance to another organization.

As a church, we donated hundreds of dollars to this organization so it could effectively serve the underprivileged.

Personally, I began to feel uncomfortable making these referrals when I knew I could help many of the people. After looking into the faces of dozens of moms and little babies and pointing toward the mission, I reached a point where I couldn't stand to make one more referral. These people didn't fit the stereotype of people living on the streets who seemed to only want money for drugs or alcohol. It was then that I came up with a crazy plan — actually, it was so crazy I felt it must have been from God. I decided to financially help *anyone* who asked me. Now this was a truly ridiculous idea since I was getting paid $70 a week as the youth minister. My parents were kind enough to pay for my education and my food and lodging, but I had to stretch this tiny paycheck to pay for my gasoline, my college road trips, and, more important, my occasional dates. There were so many people coming to the church offices looking for help, I figured there was no way I could maintain this commitment. Of course, this dawned on me only after I had promised God I would trust him in this way.

For the next several months, a remarkable thing began to happen. Just as I began to purchase groceries for a family or pay someone's gas bill, money seemed to come from out of nowhere. I have generous grandparents who always sent me some cash when each major holiday came along, but now it seemed to be more than before. I was being paid to speak at youth retreats. I discovered free ways to have fun on campus (watching movies, participating in midnight mud football, playing video games, covering the dorm bathroom floors with Vaseline, and so on). Over the course of the next year and a half, I spent about $450 of my own money meeting people's real needs.

A funny thing happened as I prepared to leave this church to get married and move to Seattle. These very wonderful people from our church in Waco threw me and Debbie a going-away party. There may be a lot of things about the South that are quirky, but one of the best things about the South is something called a "love offering." At the end of the party, our friends presented us with the cash everyone had donated for us to enjoy in our new life together. In addition to the wedding gifts they had given us at a previous wedding shower, these generous people had given us a total of $600! We were so excited and encouraged. We would need every penny we could find to move to Seattle, find jobs, and find a place to live. As we drove away, it dawned on me — God had paid me back for all the people I had helped over those several months. (Not only that, he included a very generous tip!)

It may not have been the best strategy for helping people overcome their ongoing struggle with poverty. A onetime gift doesn't erase all of the problems. I also got ripped off a few times. One woman came to the front of the church during the altar call, crying and wanting to connect with God. I prayed with her, gave her a ride home, and gave her all the cash in my wallet to help with her rent. As soon as she closed the door to her apartment, I could hear her laughing about how stupid I was to fall for her act. My strategy may have been shortsighted and naive, but I was a changed person. I discovered that God can meet the needs of others through me, and in the process he can take care of my needs as well. I realized that I could be a part of the solution to the problems I saw around me.

In spite of that experience, I know that I've had moments throughout the years when I have forgotten the poor and the oppressed. Too often my eyes are open, but I'm not seeing what should be obvious. Throughout the Scriptures, God reveals the place he has in his heart for those who are disadvantaged. As God called his people, the Israelites, to be set apart, his desire for justice and compassion was a common theme. When Israel would veer off course, the judges or the prophets would point them back toward mercy. From the mercy God offered the murderer Cain in the cities of refuge to the heavenly city described in Revelation, God has always had a heart for the city, yet too often we run away from the places of greatest need.

For a long time, I had always thought of Jesus and even Christianity as being more devoted to rural areas. But Jesus spent a great deal of time in Galilee, which was one of the most densely populated regions in the entire Roman Empire (two hundred thousand people within a fifteen-mile-by-twenty-five-mile radius).[1] Jesus wept for the city (see Luke 19:41). The Way spread through Paul's urban church planting strategy in the cities of the Roman world.

In our world, half of the urban populations of Africa, Asia, and Latin America live in slums. By 2010, 10 percent of the world's population will be children who live in the urban slums on these three continents. Right now, there are one billion urban poor in the world.[2] In the United States, there are forty million unchurched urban poor.[3] In my own city, Alhambra, California, our school district includes 25,000 students who are primarily Asian (52 percent), Latino (40 percent), and Anglo (5 percent). In this group, 67 percent of the students live below the poverty level.[4]

I've realized that I have not only failed at times to see the tremendous needs around us in our city; I have also failed to champion or even get involved with those who are already doing significant things for others. So many people in our community exert a great deal of effort that goes unnoticed. A large number of people work among those in desperate need — serving as teachers, counselors, nurses, attorneys, tutors, and doctors. Others have started businesses or responded to ongoing service opportunities, while many people and small groups volunteer a great deal of time with ministries such as Illuminate, Serve LA, Neo Underground Railroad, Awaken Humanity, the International Justice Mission, the downtown missions, and local schools. I want to do all I can to encourage those who are already serving while influencing those around me to engage in meeting the physical, spiritual, emotional, and social needs of those who are regularly overlooked.

We would be amazed at the amount of progress we can make if we reach out to serve those we deem untouchable. Just as slavery and colonialism came to an end through the efforts of passionate people, we can be a part of ending poverty. In *The End of Poverty*, Jeffrey D. Sachs makes this comment:

> Our generation is heir to two and a half centuries of economic progress. We can realistically envision a world without extreme poverty by the year 2025 because technological progress enables us to meet basic human needs on a global scale and to achieve a margin above basic needs unprecedented in history....
>
> Let the future say of our generation that we sent forth mighty currents of hope, and that we worked together to heal the world.[5]

OVERLOOKING OTHERS

Some of us have overlooked those who are in the grip of poverty. For others of us, we may disregard children, senior citizens, innovators, unreached people groups, the abused, the abusers, the victims, the imprisoned, those with whom we disagree theologically, those who are physically challenged, those who are mentally challenged, and those who are overweight. Some of us may even struggle to embrace others who might be accepted more readily.

When we love those who are overlooked or deemed untouchable by society, we should listen to them so we can learn from them the best ways to serve them, avoiding the temptation to come rushing in as a "hero" or a "knight in shining armor." At a nearby university, I was walking around during a health fair at which students were having their blood checked, receiving massages, getting healthy snacks, and so on. All around the plaza area were several booths representing different types of organizations or businesses committed to helping the students live healthier lives. One of the booths really stood out to me — the one with the hand-painted sign that read "Overeaters Anonymous." I was perplexed. If someone walked over to that booth for help, he or she would no longer be anonymous; at the same time, of the many struggles we all face, this is one that can't truly remain anonymous. The booth not only seemed to fail to attract anyone who might have wanted help; it also seemed to call attention to all of those at the health fair who should have come over. This was one of those moments when "Do to others as you would have them do to you" was worth believing and applying.

Considering our life experiences, passions, personality, and gifts, and God's leading, we should look beyond those we normally see to discover others we can serve. Debbie discovered her love for working with autistic kids as an occupational therapist. I am always amazed by Debbie and her colleagues as they demonstrate patience and selflessness in serving kids who don't or won't thank them. They find such joy in minor progress — whether it's a ten-year-old learning to tie her shoes or a six-year-old learning to use the toilet.

A friend of mine recently told of his experience adopting a little boy whose mother was in prison. He shared how his wife and kids had opened their home and their lives to a little boy who otherwise would have grown up in the foster care system. This little boy had not chosen his parents, but now he had new parents who had chosen him. My friend said that they had been thinking of adopting for years, but they were afraid of looking into the foster care system since so many of these kids have been through horrific situations. They changed their minds and proceeded after hearing a message in which Mark Driscoll, pastor of Mars Hill Church in Seattle, said, "As Christians, we are to take responsibility for the irresponsibility of others." Remarkably, my friend mentioned that the process took only eight months and a few hundred dollars to rescue this young boy and change his life forever.

As Jesus looked around at the men and women who followed him so that they could mooch a free meal, he described them as valuable and significant, as "salt and light" (see Matthew 5:13 – 14). Jesus saw the blind, those with leprosy, and the poor and met their needs. Jesus also saw those whose wallets were full but whose hearts were empty. Jesus loved them all. Jesus reached out and touched the untouchables.

FIELD NOTES

We live in a broken world — a fallen world — and the healing of our world is dependent on each one of us. We wonder why the world is so broken. How can it be that children are trafficked, forced into prostitution or into working in sweatshops to make the clothes you and I wear? How can it be that mothers still pass the HIV virus on to their unborn babies when all it takes is a $4 preventative drug to have a healthy and HIV free baby? Why is it that our young find it OK to kill each other with no remorse? Our streets and neighborhoods across America, Africa, Asia, and beyond are broken; they are filled with innocent blood.

In the midst all of this sits the church, the body of believers, busy in our own world, seated comfortably in our pews, waiting for miracles. Yet, God is saying, there are miracles all around you. There are challenges calling us everywhere— — in our own backyards, across the seas. God is waiting for us to say, "Here am I, Lord. Send me." God is looking for the opportunity to show up. He is counting on you and me to be his representatives, his hands and feet, so that when people in distress see us, it is not our human forms they see but Christ meeting their needs.

Christ was deliberate about where he went. He went where others would not want to go. He went to be with the marginalized. He touched the untouchables and the outcasts. The outcasts are not just in India or South Asia. They live among us. They are all around us. We pass them every day. They sleep on our streets; they are broken; they are affected by drugs, violence, and our own neglect. They are crying for someone to care for their orphaned children when they are gone. Who will feed their children? Who will send them to school?

The grandmother is getting weaker and weaker, yet she sits up every night not knowing how she will provide for her dozen orphaned grandchildren. Will you be the one to say, "I care. Send me, Lord"?

We need to create a church beyond the walls of the church. How can we be called the church if all we do is celebrate among ourselves and if no one from the world comes to join us? If church is not taken to the streets and the furthest corners of the world, then where is the church? Jesus said, "It is not the healthy who need a doctor, but the sick" (Matthew 9:12).

When the man lying with leprosy came to Jesus, he begged on his knees, "Lord, if you are willing, you can make me clean" (Matthew 8:2). The man knew that Jesus had the **power** to heal and make him whole, but it was the **will** to do so that was important.

A lack of food in the world is not the reason more than 1.2 billion people go to bed hungry. It is not that we as global citizens lack the resources to make sure every person in our world has shelter over their heads. Lack of treatment for HIV/AIDS is not why babies continue to be born with AIDS. It is not the reason more than 2 million children living with HIV do not have access to treatment. The reason for all this terror is simply a lack of will — the will to act, the will to make this world a better place for everyone.

How can we live with that? God is saying we must learn to do right, to seek justice, to encourage the oppressed, to defend the cause of the fatherless, and to plead the case of the widow (Isaiah 1:17).

We are called to bring healing where there is brokenness, to bring peace where there is war, to bring comfort to the afflicted, to be a voice to those whose voice cannot be heard. That is compassion.

Jesus was filled with compassion. He chose to reach out his hand and touch the man with leprosy. Jesus said, "I am willing." The true church — the one that will prevail — is the church that is willing to break the walls that divide us to reach the unreachable, to love the unlovable. Are we, as members of the church, willing?

Step by step, one action at a time, one child and one person at a time, we can make the world a better place. We can break down the walls that divide us.

Princess Kasune Zulu

Princess Kasune Zulu is the author of *Warrior Princess: Fighting for Life with Courage and Hope.* Stay in touch with her at *www.princesszulu.com* or on Facebook (warriorprincesszulu) or Twitter (PrincessKZulu).

Chapter 8

COMPASSIONATE CONSERVATIVES AND LOVING LIBERALS

Reaching across the Ideological Aisle

When we make an exclusive commitment to a political party line, we will often find ourselves failing to leave room for moments of conscience — moments when we could make a difference. I discovered this in Los Angeles when facing the issue of illegal immigration.

One day Debbie and I were shopping at the Montebello Mall when I saw an hilarious shirt hanging in the window of a Chicano store. The T-shirt was brown with a yellow traffic sign on the front that pictured a family of Pilgrims running across the street just below the word "Caution." The shirt was mocking the sign that actually exists near the border of Mexico along the freeway, which warns drivers to watch out for pedestrians by depicting the silhouettes of a man, a woman, and a pigtailed girl in the process of running. The designer of the shirt was reminding us that the original European immigrants came to Massachusetts without permission, just as is true for some Mexicans as they cross the border today.

The original traffic signs began appearing in the early 1990s after dozens of undocumented immigrants had been killed trying to cross the freeway on foot. Almost one hundred deaths took place within a five-year time frame. Those responsible for safety on our highways in California first introduced signs that read "Caution: Watch for People Crossing Road." Unfortunately, drivers failed to pay attention to the wordy warning. As a result, an artist was chosen to design a sign that would protect both those who were crossing by foot over the freeway and those who were driving along the freeway.

The signs immediately created controversy. A story in the *San Diego Tribune* summed it up: "Some Latinos felt insulted by the face-less silhouettes, which they found reminiscent of animal-crossing signs. Anti-illegal immigration advocates were angry that a state agency would be trying to protect people who had broken the law. Some people feared the signs would be misread as indicating safe places to cross."[1]

Not knowing the history behind the sign and thinking that the teens in East LA would enjoy my hip new shirt, I bought it and wore it to the next youth group event. Before I even had a chance to bask in the responses of the students, one of the moms saw me and came up to me. She did not like my shirt one bit. She was stunned that I would wear a shirt that made light of the struggles of so many people who were trying to find a better life. I pointed out that the goal of the shirt was actually to communicate that almost every American here emigrated from somewhere else. In fact, this was the reason the family was wearing Pilgrim attire, including the father with the tall hat. Still flustered by my decision making, she noted that from a distance the hat looked like a sombrero.

In the post – September 11th world, the majority of conservative evangelical Christians feel that the United States government should enforce the current immigration laws and make it more difficult for people to enter our country. Some deeply religious Christians have even created their own security brigades that "protect our borders" from undocumented immigrants. Unfortunately, this stance does not take into account some of the historical realities of our south-western states.

Present-day Los Angeles was originally inhabited by Native Americans. In the sixteenth century, Spain claimed most of the western parts of what is now the United States. In the late eighteenth century, Mexican settlers under the rule of the Spanish government formed a township and named the area *El Pueblo de Nuestra Señora la Reina de los Angeles del Río de Porciúncula* ("The Town of Our Lady the Queen of the Angels on the River Porciúncula"). The name evolved and simplified to become "Los Angeles." In 1821 Mexico gained its independence from Spain; thus, Los Angeles became a part of Mexico's territory. Just over 150 years ago, in 1847, during the Mexican-American war, the United States took control of Los Angeles after the Battle of Rio San Gabriel.

Los Angeles's population is currently right around 50 percent Latino. When some of our country's citizens assert that everyone who lives in the United States should speak English, they do not acknowledge that people have been living in this part of the world and speaking Spanish for several generations. As one of my friends put it, "If Americans didn't want people speaking Spanish, we shouldn't have moved west." During the amnesty marches of 2006, many good, upright citizens were outraged that Latinos would sing "The Star-Spangled Banner" in Spanish, failing to realize that our government commissioned this version of the song in 1918. At the same time, another friend of mine pointed out that Spanish is a European language forced on native peoples. She helped remind me just how complex these kinds of issues can be.

Currently, there are about two million illegal immigrants in California, most of whom work on farms, cook in restaurants, or help with construction projects. Without their willingness to do jobs many people aren't willing to do, our economy would suffer dramatically. Immigration from Central and South America has been more of a "don't ask, don't tell" situation. By our actions we communicate the message, "You aren't allowed to come; but if you do, here's a job." Perhaps politicians are only willing to enforce the laws that make them seem tough at the time.

Some cities have enacted what seem like harsh laws that have offended even legal immigrants. At the same time, thousands of illegal immigrants have been arrested for stealing others' identities in order to work in the United States. And, in an ironic twist, a company hired to build the fence between California and Mexico has been busted for hiring illegal immigrants. The Golden State Fence Company must pay large fines and two of their executives may face jail time. To build a wall between the United States and Mexico, as Congress approved in 2006, construction companies hire illegal immigrants in order to employ enough people to undertake such a huge task. These examples, along with many others, just confirm that we need genuine immigration reform and that we need to enforce the laws we create.

These issues remain complex and difficult to navigate. We are apt to offend someone whenever we take tough stands on all sorts of topics. If we approach political issues with sensitivity and examine them through the eyes of those most affected, perhaps we will avoid jumping on a bandwagon represented by a particular political party. As evangelicals express an increasing resistance to immigration, fearing harm at the hands of terrorists or even believing that their job security is at risk, many Latinos hear a message of exclusion. We appear to be more concerned with our politics than with our practices as followers of Christ.

The anti-immigration stance would result in the deportation of millions of people, most of whom work and pay taxes. This stance fails to address the problems faced by those who cross the borders hoping for a new life. Too often these weary travelers attempt to walk through the desert, sometimes with deadly consequences. At the same time, however, those who lean toward full amnesty diminish the efforts other immigrants have endured in order to become legal citizens of our country.

We should consider this issue beyond party lines and think in terms of what a godly response would be: "Do to others as you would have them do to you" (Luke 6:31). Or, adapted to those persons from European ethnic backgrounds who speak in favor of deporting all undocumented immigrants, the response may be, "Do to others what we would have others do to our great-great-grandparents." In his book *Race and Culture*, Thomas Sowell observes, "Of the 70 million people who emigrated from Europe over the past few centuries, nearly 50 million went to the United States — and 35 million of these arrived in just one century, from 1830 to 1930."[2] When we choose to love the foreigner in our own land, we are thanking those who accepted our ancestors.

The fact of the matter is, the Scriptures can inform and even complicate our politics, leaving honest and good people on both sides of the political aisle.

POLITICIZING JESUS

Our nation remains so politically polarized that by embracing either party we distance ourselves from roughly 50 percent of the population.

The daily news seems to report clashes in our "uncivil war" on a daily basis. Conservatives hate liberals. Liberals hate conservatives. Popular shows on cable TV and on the radio are politically charged. "The right" claims that "the left" is slanderous and "screwing up" the country, while "the left" talks of a "right-wing conspiracy." Bitterness and acrimony persist between the two groups. Since these seem to be the two most viable options during an election year, we all get lumped into one of the categories, unable to shake free of the stereotypes. If we vote for the Republicans, Democrats insist that we are saying to the world that we are pro-life, pro-war, pro – capital punishment, pro – big business, anti-environment, and anti-poor. If we vote for the Democrats, Republicans insist that we are saying that we are pro-abortion, anti-war, pro-government, pro-welfare, and pro-immigration. Either way, we end up supporting some of our values but not all of them, as Jim Wallis explained in his book *God's Politics*.[3]

Some Christians have defined the "battle" as political and have joined the cause of the Republicans. They feel they can legislate morality to protect our children from the insidious evil of liberals.

They have joined the political fight or perhaps even instigated the fight between Republicans and Democrats.

The Christian Coalition (and in earlier days the Moral Majority) has often been so vocal about its stance on issues such as abortion and homosexuality that its members have yelled themselves out of genuine conversations. Like protestors facing off across the street from each other, they yell and scream and chant to make their point, but they are unable to hear their opponents, who are doing the same thing.

So it is with those who reside to the left of center on the political spectrum. Some Christians believe that they will find the answer to the nation's problems by joining with the Democrats, who claim to be more loving and more tolerant than their conservative counterparts, yet some of the people who support a more liberal government have moved toward a more liberal theology.

I am inspired when I meet people who decided not to just get angry about an issue but to do something about it. Rather than debating with others about pro-life or pro-choice, they adopt a child, become foster parents, and mobilize others to care for babies whom some moms could not keep. We should not be content with just being moved when we watch the news or hear of something that angers us; we should be *moved to action*.

BEING RIGHT ALL THE TIME

I am a news junkie. Some may smoke a cigarette or drink a beer to relax at the end of a long day; I watch cable TV. When I have trouble slowing my mind down to sleep, I turn on the television. The blur and monotony of the images on the screen create the ideal sedative for me. Have you ever had one of those nights when you lie in bed thinking about how to make yourself stop thinking so you can finally go to sleep? On several sleepless summer nights recently, I found myself watching *The Daily Show with Jon Stewart*, which I think is the best news show (not dealing with sports) on the planet. The minds behind this masterpiece proclaim themselves to be "the one news organization with no credibility to lose." Many of my moments just before sleep nowadays are filled with interviews, stories, monologues, and montages from *The Daily Show*.

Jon Stewart makes me laugh, and I tend to laugh hardest when he makes fun of us Christians. Being able to laugh at yourself is a freeing feeling. The other night, I found myself laughing so hard that I almost woke up Debbie when Stephen Colbert described Christians as "the long-oppressed minority" because Republicans were asserting that Democrats were waging a war on Christianity. Seeing yourself through the eyes of others can bring great insight. When Jon Stewart interviewed politician Howard Dean, Dean really didn't say anything new; he just said a lot of really good things all at once:

> [Conservatives] talk about morals, but they don't do anything to help the poor. Last time I saw, helping the poor was something that was mentioned three thousand times in the Bible. I have yet to find a reference to gay marriage in the Bible. These people are obsessed with things that are not about basic core American values, and I'm sick of it and so is [sic] a lot of other people, and I am happy to stand up for them.

After the crowd erupted with applause, Jon Stewart added, "By the way, I am not through the Bible yet, so don't tell me how it ends." Later Dean described the philosophy of the Democratic community as " 'Love thy neighbor as thyself,' and you don't get to choose your neighbors."[4]

Howard Dean may not be the best public speaker around, but he summarized a lot of what we as Christians need to hear. Sadly, the world is often more aware of what and whom Christians hate rather than knowing and appreciating us for whom and how we love.

During a visit to Texas to see family and friends one recent summer, Debbie described to several people how much she enjoyed living on the West Coast. She told of how much she genuinely enjoyed living in a rather liberal environment. We have organic stores like Trader Joe's, great health care for kids with special needs, and friends from a variety of diverse backgrounds. She likes the authenticity of the people she meets. They never try to hide how they live from those around them.

When she finished her diatribe on the benefits of living in a liberal land, those in the room were shocked. I am sure they wondered what had happened to the girl who grew up going to a private Christian school where secular music was not allowed (unless, of course, it was country music). After a moment of stunned silence, the first question someone asked was, "When do you believe life begins?" Another person said, "Now, you actually like living there so you can change the liberals, right?"

Later during that same conversation, a person in the room suggested that Elizabeth Edwards (the wife of 2004 Democratic vice-presidential nominee John Edwards) deserved breast cancer since she was pro-abortion. This person's shocking opinion reveals what many Christians may think: too many of us think of tragedy in the life of someone who disagrees with us as a good thing; too many of us applaud God's judgment as just giving people what they deserve.

No one could believe that Debbie actually enjoyed her life in

La-La Land — Los Angeles, California — the land of fruits and nuts. These very good people could not understand that Debbie has friends who are gay, pro-abortion, communist, and anarchist. They felt that we should not associate with those with whom we disagree.

REMOVING THE LITMUS TEST

An Iranian woman was looking for God. Through a friend, she stumbled into a church filled with people who followed Jesus. Given her Muslim background, she wondered how she would be received. However, the warm and loving reception dispelled her fears and concerns. Not only was she drawn toward the people in this remarkably loving community; she began to become intrigued by Jesus. A personal relationship with Jesus seemed to help the men and women she had met overcome challenges and serve others in sacrificial ways. They seemed so different because they knew Jesus.

After a while, things changed dramatically. A few of her new friends within the community discovered that this intelligent and inquisitive woman was a doctor who was performing abortions. The warmth dissipated and coolness moved in. As her new friends began to debate with her about her profession, she soon felt unwelcomed and eventually left the church.

My friend who told me this story didn't know what had happened to her. So many times, a relationship with God changes how we live and who and what we value. However, I fear that she walked away from Jesus, thinking that if she wanted to know him personally, she had to make certain changes *first*.

Too often we make a person's stance on political issues a litmus test for whether a relationship can develop. As a result, if people don't believe as we do, we push them further and further away, diminishing our ability to influence both other Christians who have different values and those who do not claim to follow Christ.

This is a common theme among even the more outspoken evangelicals. In October 2005, the National Association of Evangelicals supported a stance declaring that global warming is caused by humans and needs to be addressed. Some of these well-known and well-respected pastors, including Rick Warren, author of the runaway bestseller *The Purpose Driven Life*, were ridiculed and maligned by more conservative Christians for agreeing with "far-left environmentalists."

Ironically, during the summer heat wave of 2006, Pat Robertson, one of the outspoken critics, changed his mind. An article posted on Reuters.com titled "Heat Makes Pat Robertson a Global Warming 'Convert'" reports:

> Conservative Christian broadcaster Pat Robertson said on Thursday the wave of scorching temperatures across the United States has converted him into a believer in global warming.
>
> "We really need to address the burning of fossil fuels," Robertson said on his "700 Club" broadcast. "It is getting hotter, and the icecaps are melting and there is a buildup of carbon dioxide in the air."

After the heat index reached 115 degrees in Robertson's part of the world, he mentioned on his television program that the heat wave was "the most convincing evidence I've seen on global warming in a long time."

The article continues, "Last year, Robertson said natural disasters affecting the globe, including hurricanes Katrina and Rita that wrecked the U.S. Gulf Coast, might be signs that the biblical apocalypse was nearing."

Perhaps we should all switch to hybrid cars and use less electricity to save the ozone layer and help avoid global warming, or maybe fears about global warming are much like our fears about the Y2K bug. Regardless, we should all consider examining each issue in a way that is independent of any particular political party, and then willingly dialogue with those who often disagree with us. Robertson's initial response of criticizing other Christian leaders for particular points on which they agree with liberals implies that we should avoid all contact with others unless they agree with us in every way. If we took this approach, the pool of people with whom we could network or partner would dwindle to a small puddle.

When we share the same outcome goals with those who differ from us, partnership remains a powerful option. As long as we do not compromise our own values and beliefs in the process, we should look for opportunities to dialogue and even team up with others across the political spectrum. Jesus was deemed guilty by association, as the religious leaders referred to him as "a glutton and a drunkard, a friend of... sinners" (Matthew 11:19); therefore, we should be willing to work with others with whom we disagree in order to accomplish something noble — and to develop meaningful relationships as well.

A few years ago, one of our volunteer staff members suggested we get involved in "Big Sunday," a one-day "clean up the city" initiative founded and led by Temple Israel of Hollywood. One of the leaders of the event mentioned that they were surprised we were willing to help, since so few evangelical churches had ever shown interest. In 2006 the mayor of LA, Antonio Villaraigosa, teamed up with Big Sunday. We had approximately thirty thousand people volunteering at more than two hundred nonprofit sites during this "Annual Day of Service." How could we miss this kind of an opportunity to make an impact on our communities?

When we step into partnerships with those with whom we disagree in order to fight poverty, clean up our cities, fight injustice, and tackle issues we cannot solve on our own, we discover that we have an unlimited number of potential partners to help us make positive and lasting changes in our world.

History teaches us that it is possible to change the world from the ground up. We can learn this lesson from Ghandi and Martin Luther King Jr., and also we can see it displayed in the biblical story of Nineveh. The eighth-century BC prophet Jonah arrived in Nineveh and delivered his message:

> Jonah obeyed the word of the LORD and went to Nineveh. Now Nineveh was a very large city; it took three days to go through it. Jonah began by going a day's journey into the city, proclaiming, "Forty more days and Nineveh will be overthrown." The Ninevites believed God. They declared a fast, and all of them, from the greatest to the least, put on sackcloth.
>
> When the news reached the king of Nineveh, he rose from his throne, took off his royal robes, covered himself with sackcloth and sat down in the dust. Then he issued a proclamation in Nineveh ..."
>
> Jonah 3:3 – 7

After all of the Ninevites had turned to the Lord, the king felt the need to make a proclamation. (It was almost as though he wanted it to seem like it was *his* idea!) This radical transformation began with the people and moved upward. The king was the last to know. We need men and women who follow God and hold to strong moral values finding their places of influence in the political world, but systemic and long-lasting transformation comes from the grass roots and moves upward.

Often, whether we realize it or not, we assume that real issues can only be solved politically. As we study the history books, we hear of the Emancipation Proclamation, the Civil War, and the Thirteenth Amendment, and we assume that Abraham Lincoln and other politicians ended slavery. Ironically, however, the goal of the Civil War was the bringing back of secessionist states while allowing slavery to continue in these states. As the war took its staggering toll, public sentiment in the North and in the border states shifted. Slavery's end was no longer just a concern for abolitionists. The public accepted the idea before the legislation ever went into effect.

Lincoln understood the dynamics of what was happening and proclaimed, "With public sentiment nothing can fail; without it, nothing can succeed.... Consequently, he who holds public sentiment goes deeper than he who erects statutes or pronounces decisions."[5]

For those who have worked so hard politically and legislatively to bring about an end to abortions, if public sentiment remains divided even as the laws change, abortions would continue illegally until a shift in political power legalized them once again. To reduce abortions, people need to change their view of when life begins and see the consequences of their actions. This change would become noticeable with or without a law in the books.

We need to vote, and we need Christian men and women who work within both the Democratic Party and the Republican Party. The political arena represents a tremendous mission field filled with people who have great influence or at least a tremendous potential to influence others. More than anything, our politics should always be secondary to our practice as followers of Christ.

The apostle Paul wrote beautiful and memorable words about God's great work of reconciliation:

Therefore, remember that formerly you who are Gentiles by birth and called "uncircumcised" by those who call themselves "the circumcision" (which is done in the body by human hands) — remember that at that time you were separate from Christ, excluded from citizenship in Israel and foreigners to the covenants of the promise, without hope and without God in the world. But now in Christ Jesus you who once were far away have been brought near by the blood of Christ.

For he himself is our peace, who has made the two one and has destroyed the barrier, the dividing wall of hostility, by setting aside in his flesh the law with its commands and regulations. His purpose was to create in himself one new humanity out of the two, thus making peace, and in one body to reconcile both of them to God through the cross, by which he put to death their hostility. He came and preached peace to you who were far away and peace to those who were near. For through him we both have access to the Father by one Spirit.

Consequently, you are no longer foreigners and strangers, but fellow citizens with God's people and also members of his household, built on the foundation of the apostles and prophets, with Christ Jesus himself as the chief cornerstone.

Ephesians 2:11 – 20

Not only did those of us who follow Christ find ourselves on the wrong side of the border; Christ helped us cross over and reconciled us with those on the other side. Our allegiance belongs first and foremost to God's kingdom. Our heavenly citizenship should always guide how we live our lives and how we treat others as citizens of our country and of our world.

FIELD NOTES

Eric Bryant calls Christians to avoid building their religious convictions around their political attitudes. It's an important message. He knows that far too many Christians find a comfortable substitute for engaged and compassionate responses to world challenges in practicing sheer political loyalty. In the 1980s and 1990s, conservative Christians aligned themselves to political agendas centered on issues such as abortion, national security, and free-market capitalism. As a result, some Christians believe they accomplish their spiritual duty by arguing well-rehearsed political positions on hot-button topics. This debate-centered approach cripples rather than strengthens our Christian witness.

Because so many Christians are convinced of the moral rightness of their positions, Eric and I both know that the call to reconsider our attitudes and our actions in relation to our politics can be challenging. I've seen Christians unable to stand in the same room with others whose stance on abortion rights or same-sex marriage is different from their own. People are much quicker to change their churches than they are to change their politics. I know Christians who left their churches to join others they deem more "biblical" and have a proper approach to "discipleship" in contrast to their former pastors who failed to hold with "discernment" the correct political views. These "God-fearing" people are unwilling to create relational room for people who approach the world differently. They abandon diversity in pursuit of a social comfort that reinforces their assumptions and accentuates prejudice.

Regardless of our place on the political spectrum, we must create room in our lives for faithful people who actively question the premises of past political platforms. I like when Eric writes, "Scripture can inform and even complicate our politics, leaving honest and good people on both sides of the political aisle." Rather than crafting a rhetorical strategy for winning arguments, he believes that faithful people are called to action from all sides of the political spectrum. Eric urges us to take practical steps in engaging the dilemmas faced by real people. He believes we should put our hands and our hearts to labor on behalf of the poor and the oppressed. Even more, Eric believes that we need to remove the litmus test of judging a person's spirituality on the basis of their political convictions. We need to restore a profound sense of hospitality that truly welcomes the political stranger — that person who seems so foreign and different to us — and join together as part of a multifaceted spiritual community.

In order to create that hospitality, we need to get out of a mentality that exaggerates political agreement as a mask for being energized by others who share similar points of view. Such a rallying mentality leads to hateful riots that demonize others as a means to bolster a fragile unity. In contrast, we need to recognize ourselves as a diverse people of faith who are confronted daily with real-world issues that are challenging, complex, and ever-changing. It is time to reevaluate our relationship to positions that have claimed to represent the Christian faith.

With the fall of the Berlin wall — and more recently the fall of the Twin Towers — we find ourselves in a transformed global environment and a need to rethink standard solutions offered by previous generations. This is not a time for a wide-eyed, white-fisted stance based on a foundation of false convictions. Instead, we are compelled as responsible adults to think carefully about current issues and evaluate not only how they affect our own political preferences but also the global community in which we live. Our uncertainties should move us to solicit various points of view and creatively engage a broader spectrum of voices and perspectives to forge new outlooks for a largely unanticipated future. Faithfulness today leads toward a teachable stance willing to meet new challenges. We must redefine our faithful responses with each new context.

In the end, the most practical action we can take is to put down our voter registration guides, avoid confusing political passions with intimate bonds, and stop trying to isolate changeless convictions in a changing world. The future of the mission of Christ does not depend on our politics but on our holding firm a conviction that people are more important than a platform. Let us stop defining who gets our attention merely on the basis of their sympathy for our political views. Instead, let us become truly openhearted, hopeful people who are characterized by hospitality rather than hostility and who readily give a warm embrace to the multiplicity of political orientations. And let our faith lead us to learning and accommodating with others to the ongoing fluctuations of the world as they come.

Dr. Gerardo Marti

Gerardo is professor of sociology at Davidson College and the author of *A Mosaic of Believers, Hollywood Faith,* and *Worship across the Racial Divide.* He is active in several research partnerships, and his broad interests include worship and the arts, racial and ethnic diversity, religious innovation, and congregational responses to social change. Gerardo blogs at *praxishabitus.blogspot.com* and can be followed on Twitter (praxishabitus).

Chapter 9

LOTS OF SEX IN THE CITY

Engaging Others in a Post – Sexual Revolution World

For students, the end of a quarter at school is always a joyous time. Debbie had been laboring intensely for several months in her occupational therapy classes at the University of Washington. She was part of a group of twenty-five students who had been chosen from a group of several hundred. These students had been working hard studying genetics, kinesiology, chemistry, and biology — and they were ready to celebrate.

Karen, one of Debbie's classmates, invited all of the students and their families and friends to come over to celebrate their survival. The thought of talking about knee joints, hyperextension, sensory integration, and all of the other big words these students were learning was horrible. Even more unsettling, Karen lived with her girlfriend, Carrie. Yes, I said it. Girlfriend. Not the "let's trade makeup and talk about hot boys" girlfriend. More like the "more than a friend" friend. I found myself hoping the other students were going to be there. I was not prepared for a double date with lesbians.

As we drove over to Karen's house, I was astonished to see that most of the classmates were already there. My fear of a double date abated; now my thoughts turned to how I could endure the party. As we entered the house, the noise was deafening. Everyone was talking loudly and all at once. They were acting like old friends who had survived some tragedy together — and perhaps they had! They were discussing their vivid memories of the cadaver lab, reports, papers, and professors as though they were extraordinarily fascinating to those of us not in the program. I resolved to work on my attitude and to enjoy the gathering.

Karen greeted us soon after we arrived. My plan was to find the husbands or boyfriends who had been dragged there so I could commiserate with them about how hard the occupational therapy program was for me. Karen was hindering my attempts to find the men. But I had to admit, I really liked Karen. She was bubbly and effervescent. She had a contagious laugh and a huge smile that revealed very white teeth. She was truly enjoyable. It was hard for me to fathom that she was gay.

I didn't know much about what it meant to be gay. I just remember being told as I was growing up that it was a horrible sin. Being gay seemed to be more than a lifestyle; it included an agenda attempting to make us all gay. ("Agenda" sounds like such a horrible word. I didn't want to be on anyone's agenda.) My experiences with gay people had always fit into the stereotypes. The guys I knew who were gay were either trying desperately to overcome their gay desires or busily recruiting others.

Karen was the first gay woman I had ever met. She was also the first gay person who didn't seem to fit the two stereotypes stuck in my mind. She was neither distraught nor proselytizing. I couldn't figure out why she was so nice. My preconception was that all lesbians were like tennis legend Martina Navratilova. I was expecting Karen to have big biceps, a deep voice, and a mean backhand. Instead, she was just as nice as some of the people I had known in church during my childhood. Actually, she was nicer than many of them.

A few other classmates began arriving as Karen continued sharing with Debbie and me about her life before occupational therapy school. After a few moments, I saw an opportunity to sneak away without being rude. In addition to finding the husbands and boyfriends, I wanted to find the food. Going to parties with strangers is almost worthwhile, depending on the quality of the food being offered. I came across a table in the kitchen, which was filled with all sorts of delectable dishes, including little chimichangas. I love chimichangas! The little ones are even better since they mean more fried tortilla per square inch than larger ones. Karen sure knew how to treat her guests!

I wolfed down a couple of chimichangas as I stood at the table, and then I remembered that I was a grown-up married guy at a party with adults. I should put my food on an actual plate rather than pretending that the platter was all mine. After discovering I could fit five little chimichangas on a plate (even leaving enough room for the salsa), I turned around and saw Carrie looking at me. I almost dropped my plate. This was Karen's girlfriend, but it was obvious that she was more like Karen's boyfriend. She had the large biceps and deep voice. I hoped she didn't have a mean backhand.

Since my mouth was full of chimichanga, Carrie spoke first. "Are you Debbie's husband?"

"Uh, yes," I stammered as I tried to quickly chew and swallow that golden-brown, delicious bite. "Are you Karen's — ?"

My mind stopped working. I didn't know what to call her! I paused, continuing to chew my food. I started thinking through all of the politically correct words to describe Carrie. Spouse? (No, they couldn't be legally married.) Girlfriend? (Sounded too young and teenagery.) Boyfriend? (Didn't seem right since she did not have male anatomical parts.) Partner? (Sounded too much like a business arrangement.) Mate? (Absolutely impossible.) Lover? (Way too vivid and descriptive.) Roommate? (Not warm enough.) I knew she knew I knew.

She got tired of waiting, or perhaps she simply had mercy on me. Before I could come up with an appropriate word to finish my question, she answered, "Yes, I am. We've been together for the past six years." Whew! I didn't have to reveal my ignorance when it came to lesbian nomenclature.

Since I had made such a great first impression, I was surprised that she continued the conversation.

"I imagine you're as relieved as I am that this quarter is over. Could you believe how much work they made them do? Karen hardly came to bed the past two weeks!"

She had me, and then she lost me. They *had* been working really hard. My wife and I *had* hardly seen each other in weeks, but I couldn't get past the fact she had just admitted she slept in the same bed as her — whatever she's called. I don't know if she discerned on me any sort of facial expression that may have betrayed my shock and disbelief, but she continued on. "When I came up with the idea for this party, I wanted to invite all the families over too, since we have to do so much work just to get them through this!"

Before I had a chance to digest the fact that she was considering herself to be in Karen's family, I found myself blurting out, "You're right! I've been picking up fast food every night this past week. I love Taco Bell, but even bean burritos can get old after a while."

For the next fifteen minutes, Carrie and I commiserated with each other. Karen and Debbie had both been neglecting us. Neither one had been cooking or cleaning or setting aside any time for us. Both of them were coming home wanting to practice some of their new occupational therapy proprioception techniques on us (I still have no idea what this means). Both seemed to think they had contracted one of the illnesses, conditions, syndromes, or maladies they had been studying — apparently a somewhat common problem for medical students. We each had to help convince them that just because they started coughing, it didn't mean they had tuberculosis, or that even though they had a headache, it was because of a lack of sleep, not because they had contracted meningitis. In addition to our similar struggles, I discovered that Carrie also loved the chimichangas. She had picked them out specially for this party.

Debbie and Karen entered the kitchen at this point. Karen mentioned that the flower arrangement decorating the table was a gift from Carrie congratulating her on the completion of the quarter. Debbie blurted out, "I wish Eric would have been so thoughtful. His way of congratulating me was agreeing to come to this party!"

My lips formed a nervous smile as I took a bite of chimichanga number four. Karen's lover threw this party; Debbie's lover barely even came to the party. Debbie followed up this wonderful revelation with a dig of her elbow into my side as she wondered aloud, "Eric, why *didn't* you buy me flowers? This arrangement is beautiful!"

I felt my neck getting hot. I wasn't angry; I was embarrassed. It was clear that Debbie felt Carrie made a better husband than I did. How can I compete with a woman when it comes to being sensitive and caring? It seemed as though Debbie wanted a husband who thought more like a woman.

Others came into the kitchen and commented on the beautiful flowers Carrie had bought for Karen. In spite of my embarrassment and frustration, I eventually let it go. Karen and Carrie both intrigued me and confused me. They were both so normal. They did not fit my view of what homosexuals were like. I really enjoyed my time at their house. I felt welcomed.

Just before leaving the party, I found myself standing next to Carrie as Karen and Debbie were saying farewell. It was one of those awkward moments when you aren't sure whether you should start another conversation, since the other conversation may be ending any moment. I always hate leaving anywhere with Debbie. It's almost impossible for me to distinguish between when she is almost ready to say good-bye and when she is still in the middle of a story. Carrie broke the silence.

"So, Eric, what do you do for a living?"

I never liked answering that question, especially in Seattle. When I would answer this question in Texas, I could tell that people respected me. I thought about a few alternative ways to answer Carrie's question — that I work with disadvantaged teenagers, or that I helped to lead a nonprofit organization. It quickly dawned on me that the timing of my response had extended past what is considered polite, so I finally just told her the truth.

"I'm a pastor at a church called The Anchor."

If I had wanted a way out of the conversation earlier that evening when I first met Carrie, I could have introduced myself as Pastor

Eric. She undoubtedly would have snatched up her own chimi-changa and made a beeline for the living room. Her jaw dropped as she stumbled to follow up my response. Out of the corner of my eye, I noticed Debbie hugging Karen. This moment was almost over. Trying to extend mercy to her, I quickly asked, "So what do you do?"

"I'm a gynecologist."

This time *my* jaw dropped.

DOES GOD HATE FAGS?

I have heard my fair share of bad words in my day. As a junior high kid, I used to try to use all of them. One of the favorite words my posse of friends would use to demean each other was the word "fag." It was the absolute worst put-down for us guys. Honestly, I think as junior highers and high schoolers, my buddies and I would rather have had people mock our moms than question our sexuality. We tried to act as macho as possible all the time, especially when we were in the showers after football practice. As a late bloomer await-ing my first armpit hair, I became Houdini after football practice, sneaking away before the coach could find me and make me jump in the shower. Extra deodorant and a wet paper towel for my face were enough for me. The last experience I ever wanted was to stand naked in a shower with a bunch of guys who were accusing each other of loving other guys. I would rather smell funky in second-hour geography.

In my efforts to always appear to be a nice guy when I was around adults, I learned to be bilingual, speaking English around my parents, Sunday school teachers, our pastor, and teachers at school but using suburban street English around my buddies. If ever I found myself speaking suburban street English around adults, I had alternative words to help me cover for myself — you know, all of those "almost swearwords" that seem to be OK to say, even though they are simply a letter or two away from the original — words like "shoot," "dadgummit," "freakin'," "dang," "heck," and so on. The word "fag" was dangerous, for there was no close replacement. I remember trying to think through my available explanations in case I ever got caught calling someone a "fag." Ironically, even if I had been caught, I doubt I would have gotten in trouble for uttering a word that demeans homosexuals; I would have been rebuked for suggesting that someone was a homosexual. (In either case, I knew that explaining that I was calling another junior high guy the slang word for "cigarette" would not get me out of trouble.) Finally, I had an epiphany. It was impossible to get in trouble, for I had a perfectly plausible and airtight alibi: I had learned the word "fag" from Christians — some of whom I had seen holding a picket sign that blared in all caps, "GOD HATES FAGS!"

Over the years, some Christians have expressed their opinion of homosexuality in quite clear and unambiguous tones. These well-meaning Christians protest against people they do not know, people they fear because of their lifestyles. Homosexuals whose family members are Christians, and even homosexuals who consider themselves to be Christians, ask their heterosexual Christian parents or heterosexual Christian friends to try to understand them, yet many Christians are revolted. They don't *want* to understand. They want to keep gays and lesbians as far away as possible. In fact, more often than not, Christians see homosexuals as the enemy and vice versa.

Homophobia is an irrational fear of those who are living a homosexual lifestyle. Those with the mildest hint of homophobia alienate themselves from homosexuals, thereby eliminating their ability to befriend and perhaps even influence those with whom they disagree. The harshest form of homophobia leads toward more than just ridicule and prejudice directed against gays and lesbians; some homosexuals have experienced violence (sometimes resulting in death) at the hands of extremists. Some of those extremists would claim moral superiority over their victims. These ridiculous instigators of hatred and violence toward those with whom they disagree idolize criminals such as Paul Hill and Eric Rudolph, ideologues who killed doctors who performed abortions. Almost all Christians would denounce these tactics as obscene and even horrific.

Sadly, many of us Christians have not gone the extra mile to show the world that Christ loved all people. The world outside of Christianity usually lumps us into the same corral as murderers of homosexuals and bombers of abortion clinics. It becomes a persistent problem for us when we choose not to associate with people who live differently from the way we live or believe differently from the way we believe; when we keep others at a distance, we don't give them an opportunity to get to know who we really are. Instead, huddling together, some Christians link arms with each other and form a tight, impenetrable circle against the world, lobbing from afar verbal grenades at those who do not share our values, making sure none of the shrapnel touches us. As a result, once again the world is more aware of what and whom Christians hate rather than knowing us for whom and how we love.

Thanks to Mickey Mouse, I felt this rather acutely when we lived in Seattle. In the 1990s Disney decided to offer health insurance to same-sex partners of their employees, and many evangelical Christians did not like it at all. The Southern Baptist denomination specifically mobilized its gigantic constituency to action, observing that Disney cannot claim to be family-friendly while supporting same-sex health coverage. In 1997 Southern Baptists chose to boycott

Disney. If everything went according to script, Disney would change its policies and Southern Baptists would become more prudent when it came to spending money on entertainment. (A couple of years later, Debbie and I moved to Los Angeles, where we met some people at our church who worked at Disney. In fact, they were leading a Bible study there with other employees, some of whom were not yet followers of Christ. I suppose they hadn't gotten the memo about the boycott.)

One of my friends in Seattle had been struggling with his sexual identity. His honesty with me about his struggle seemed tenuous. We had been friends for a while, but now I was afraid his trust would evaporate. He knew that I belonged to a Southern Baptist church, a fact for which he often mocked me. Even in Seattle, the SBC boycott of Disney over the issue of homosexuality came through loud and clear on the news. I knew that our conversations about God and life and choices and being gay were at great risk. I thought they would come to an end. Thankfully, I was wrong. He looked past the fact that I was Southern Baptist and saw me as a human being, as a friend. He chose not to lump me into a stereotype, or even into a caricature.

I wanted to treat him the same way. Admittedly, hearing him talk about his homosexual encounters freaked me out at first. In some ways, I felt tricked. He was a friend before I knew of his alternative lifestyle. Had I known how he lived his life at night, I probably never would have continued to hang out. Once he began to open up about his life, I wanted to walk away from his friendship. I wanted to introduce a "don't ask, don't tell" policy for our times at Starbucks until I realized he wanted help. He needed to be able to share what was happening in his life and in his mind and in his spirit. Many times I had no idea how to relate or how to encourage him, so I would just listen. I would ask him questions. When he would ask for advice, I would be honest about my thoughts. I would point him toward God and the Scriptures, asking him to reflect on what he was sensing that God was saying.

Thankfully, my friend worked through his struggles. Some people in the same situation have chosen to end their lives rather than continue on their journey, confused and misunderstood. Instead, he chose a radical path. The last time we talked, he was helping in a ministry that serves primarily senior adults. He was focused more on helping others than on searching for someone with whom to have sex. He sees himself more as a spiritual person than as just a sexual one, having made a choice to remain celibate. He has chosen to live his life in a way that matches his convictions as a follower of Christ. I'm glad that I didn't label him a sinner, that I wasn't unwilling to spend time with him, afraid of what others might think or reviled by his behavior. I would have missed a fantastic friendship, as well as the opportunity to learn more about myself. When left to my own devices, I am judgmental and uncaring. He allowed me to discover a glimpse of Christ's heart in the way he treated me. I hope I was able to do the same for him.

All denominations have a checkered past when it comes to loving. The Southern Baptist Convention is no exception. (My intent is not to slam Southern Baptists; it's just that I know them so well, having been involved in Southern Baptist churches my entire life.) It is undeniable that Southern Baptists have done many good things down through the years, but I'm not convinced that boycotting Disney was one of them. (Over the past several years, fans of the boycott credit their efforts for keeping Disney's stock price from rising, as well as for the departure of CEO Michael Eisner. The boycott ended just in time for the release of the film adaptation of C. S. Lewis's *The Lion, the Witch, and the Wardrobe*. Coincidence? You decide.)

When we point our finger at homosexuals and claim moral

superiority, we act as though we have it all together. We act as though the struggles we heterosexual Christians have with pornography, adultery, lust, and divorce are not as bad. Some parents act as though they don't mind if their son is sexually active in junior high or high school, just as long as he is involved with a girl. But we are *all* sinners. We are all far away from experiencing the ideal life God has in mind for us.

Sadly, when we push away those who have homosexual tendencies, we eliminate opportunities to show Christ's love, much less to influence others. The truth is, allowing someone to come into and be a part of our community is not the same as allowing them to lead. We should have a wide door when it comes to attendance and participation while we are engaged in serving those who visit and helping them to discover a relationship with God. We need to put the onus on those who are leaning toward homosexuality to reject us rather than vice versa. I have heard too many stories of churches that pushed struggling teenagers out of their church doors and into the arms of those who actively live homosexual lifestyles.

At the annual Hollywood Halloween parade, many gay men, lesbians, and transvestites dress up and walk up and down the street in their scary costumes. Apparently, angry Christian protestors show up at this parade every year. It is a small but vocal bunch. A friend of mine who went last year told of a new group of Christians who had "crashed the party." Rather than holding up signs that proclaimed judgment, these men and women lifted a giant cross that contained signs declaring, "We're Sorry," and "Free Hugs." Not sure how to respond, a line of homosexuals began to approach this group who had adopted this odd method. Rather than engaging others in debates or even in dialogue, these "protestors" delivered what they had promised — free hugs to many surprised and receptive people.

HATING THE SINNER, LOVING THE SIN

Even we Christians are captivated by the bizarre. Our minds go into overdrive as we hear the salacious details of a scandal — the more heinous and the more sexual the better. Stories of a husband leaving his wife for another man or vice versa seem to be among the most shocking yet most interesting. Just as spectators who slow down create traffic jams as they crane their necks to catch a glimpse at the carnage on the side of the road, we seek to discover the details (so we can know how to "pray more effectively" for those involved). We seem to have no problem hating the sinner, yet somehow we often seem to love the sin. Scandalous news quickly travels among us in the name of prayer requests, even as we try to avoid participating in the painful healing process necessary for those involved in the scandal.

Sex "sells" because we are obsessed with sex. Magazines, television, the Internet, and movies show pictures and images of sexual scenes because our world sees sex as a great escape from life's struggles. As a result, this society is filled with people who have chosen to live by a different set of standards — those who live a homosexual lifestyle as well as those who engage in sex before or outside of marriage. President Bill Clinton's reframing of the definition of sex opened the way for more people, including teenagers, to consider their exploits as acceptable. The existence of strip clubs, pornography, and promiscuous relationships reveals a brokenness within our hearts, which we try to fix with these dangerous and destructive adventures. Sadly, I am not simply referring to those who do not follow Christ. Those who call themselves Christians and those who do not — both seem to make similar decisions sexually. The only difference would be the conviction of wrongdoing that some Christians feel.

Knowing how to respond to those who are sexually active outside of marriage is an important skill we need to develop. First, let's consider our response to those who choose sexual activity other than what evangelicals see as appropriate. How should we respond to non-Christians with regard to this issue?

I imagine most Christians would believe wholeheartedly in the phrase "love the sinner and hate the sin." Yet many of us as Christians have not gone the extra mile to show the world that Christ does, in fact, love the sinner. Jesus seemed to show no hesitation whatsoever to befriend those with whom he did not agree. Wherever Jesus went in his days on earth, many people were drawn to him. Others despised him. Many others were confused by him. Generally, those who despised Jesus were those who were deeply religious. They hated the way Jesus would fraternize with "sinners," yet those who were drawn to him tended to be those very same "sinners." Tax collectors, thieves, immoral people, and those who were demon-possessed all redirected their lives to follow Jesus. Jesus gained a reputation among the religious leaders as "a glutton and a drunkard" (Matthew 11:19) because he spent so much time with immoral people.

Paul described behaviors and attitudes of the sinful nature — the part of us that pulls away from God. To the Corinthian believers he wrote the following:

> Do you not know that wrongdoers will not inherit the kingdom of God? Do not be deceived: Neither the sexually immoral nor idolaters nor adulterers nor male prostitutes nor practicing homosexuals nor thieves nor the greedy nor drunkards nor slanderers nor swindlers will inherit the kingdom of God. And that is what some of you were. But you were washed, you were

sanctified, you were justified in the name of the Lord Jesus
Christ and by the Spirit of our God.

1 Corinthians 6:9 – 11

Christians are quick to point to the descriptions "sexually
immoral," "adulterers," "male prostitutes," and "practicing homosexuals." With great speed, we apply this passage to others we do
not know or like; however, we must not ignore the parts of the Bible
we do not like and claim the rest as true. Think of all the people you
know who would consider themselves to be Christians. What percentage of these people have gotten drunk or stolen something? Of
those you have not included in that group, what percentage have ever
slandered another person or found themselves caught up in greed?
Although the consequences of sin remain different, all sin separates
us from the ideal life God has in mind for us. All of us have come
up short, and without God we would have neither the desire nor the
strength to change.

Jesus reveals a very different approach from the judgmental one
we often embrace. Jesus actually befriended people on the fringe of
society. He embraced the people the religious leaders loved to hate.
Early in the morning, the religious leaders thought they had found
a way to trap Jesus. Creeping around and peering into the bedrooms
of some of the more notorious women in town, they found their bait.
Dragging an adulterous woman in front of Jesus, they demanded that
their moral legislation be followed. They knew that Jesus would not
condone her behavior; therefore, he would have to participate in her
stoning, an act that would prove that his teaching about showing love
to others was wrong. The gospel writer John tells what happened:

At dawn he [Jesus] appeared again in the temple courts,
where all the people gathered around him, and he sat down to

teach them. The teachers of the law and the Pharisees brought in a woman caught in adultery. They made her stand before the group and said to Jesus, "Teacher, this woman was caught in the act of adultery. In the Law Moses commanded us to stone such women. Now what do you say?" They were using this question as a trap, in order to have a basis for accusing him.

But Jesus bent down and started to write on the ground with his finger. When they kept on questioning him, he straightened up and said to them, "Let any one of you who is without sin be the first to throw a stone at her." Again he stooped down and wrote on the ground.

At this, those who heard began to go away one at a time, the older ones first, until only Jesus was left, with the woman still standing there. Jesus straightened up and asked her, "Woman, where are they? Has no one condemned you?"

"No one, sir," she said.

"Then neither do I condemn you," Jesus declared. 'Go now and leave your life of sin."

John 8:2 – 11

What do you think Jesus had written on the ground? Perhaps it was a message in Aramaic: "Love your neighbor." Perhaps the accusers began to walk away as Jesus began writing their secret sins in the dirt. More important than his artistic endeavor was his response: he saved her from execution on moral grounds. Rather than condemning her, he showed compassion and love while calling her to live a transformed life. Too often we relate to others in the opposite order. Through our actions, we communicate, "We will love you when you change," rather than Jesus' approach, which was, "I will love you whether or not you change, and if you want to change, I will show you how."

Some time ago, Joan and Mark began attending our church. They had been living together for a while, yet they both felt drawn to look for something spiritual. Joan's sordid past had included many different attempts to find God or Truth through Wicca, ashrams, and Yoga, as well as several other philosophies. Mark had abandoned the Christianity of his youth. After attending a Sunday gathering, they began to get involved by attending retreats, a small group, and the actors' workshop, while developing friendships with many new people. We all knew about their living situation, but, more important, we all knew that they were not followers of Christ.

Miraculously, Joan and Mark both chose to follow Christ over the course of the next few months. Soon they became engaged, and they wanted to join our volunteer staff. When we got together for the first meeting in that process, we had a great conversation about their new relationships with Christ. They both truly desired to serve God and serve others. You could imagine how surprised I was afterward to discover that on their registration cards each had listed the same address. I prepared myself for a difficult conversation the next time we got together since they were still living together as an engaged couple, even though they were now followers of Christ.

The time came to meet, and I tried a subtle approach. "Have you found a place to live after your wedding ceremony?" I asked. They began talking about the apartment they had listed on their registration cards. As they shared that Mark was staying on a friend's couch until the big day, I was relieved. Like other couples in our community, their new life with Jesus had led them to spend time apart to honor God with their relationship and to help them reach their friends, who still could not believe the change in their lives.

Since they began following Christ, Mark and Joan never cease to amaze me. Not only did they choose to abstain sexually during their engagement; they have worked through the pain and brokenness from their pasts, endured a challenging pregnancy with faith (giving birth to a beautiful little girl named Harper), and continued to sacrifice in order to serve those in their lives who have tremendous needs.

Over and over again, I have discovered that once a person truly encounters Christ, the Spirit of God, the encouraging words of others who follow Christ, and a desire to reach his or her friends guide the new believer to live a truly transformed life. When we are serving and loving Christians who find themselves struggling with sexual choices, a similar approach leads to similar results. Since God offers a great deal of kindness to help move us toward repentance (see Romans 2:4), we should pursue the practice of the same style.

We all need God. Even on our best day, when we exert our own maximum effort, we cannot get past our wickedness. None of us will inherit the kingdom of God as rightful heirs. Our only hope is to be adopted into God's family through Christ's death on the cross and his resurrection from the dead. He alone has the power to cleanse us. Christ offers hope and transformation for all of us. We all can find forgiveness and transformation, no matter which of those descriptions on Paul's list describe our past or present actions.

At times I have discovered that those who call themselves Christians yet live as though they are not may truly be disconnected from God. They may need to discover what a genuine relationship with God means. Other times, Christians who have fallen away need someone who is willing to care enough to be involved in their lives. When we care enough to invest in the lives of those who live dangerously, we will be amazed at their willingness to hear our words. Most people who follow Christ acknowledge a need to change and their need for help. In these moments, we can help them, just as others have helped us. When we judge others from a distance, we miss our opportunity to help them.

On the rare occasion when a believer continues to make destructive choices a habit, the Scriptures, through the apostle Paul, give us this insight:

> I wrote to you in my letter not to associate with sexually immoral people — not at all meaning the people of this world who are immoral, or the greedy and swindlers, or idolaters. In that case you would have to leave this world. But now I am writing you that you must not associate with any who claim to be fellow believers but are sexually immoral or greedy, idolaters or slanderers, drunkards or swindlers. With such persons do not even eat.
>
> **1 Corinthians 5:9 – 11**

Paul was writing to a group of believers who had allowed a man who was sleeping with "his father's wife" (1 Corinthians 5:1) to continue living in that relationship! We know we are to serve and restore those who are in sin, but there are extreme instances when we should separate ourselves from a person who claims to follow Christ yet refuses to stop destructive patterns. Paul implored the leaders at Corinth to care enough for this man to engage in a difficult conversation to help him see how destructive this situation truly was. Paul encouraged the Corinthians to take drastic measures. Even then, the entire purpose of church discipline is so that a person will change his or her mind and actions and return to the community once again.

What do lesbian gynecologists, homosexuals, Mickey Mouse, sexually active persons, Christians, and Southern Baptists have in common? We all need help. We all need love, and we all need friendship. We can help others change through meaningful conversations in the context of meaningful relationships.

FIELD NOTES

The past few decades have seen American Christians going in two different directions. One group in the church regularly pits scorched-earth, "come out and be separate" teaching against another group proposing the "love your neighbor as yourself" command of Jesus as paramount. Some want to save America, while others want to save Americans. Many believers have been taught that we should shun nonbelievers, since any friendship with them might cause us to stumble and fall into sin ourselves. The response is to construct a protective boundary that keeps us at a safe distance from those "living in sin." It results in a subculture of churched people who are the equivalent of evangelical Amish.

While it is important for Christians to have and proclaim the moral standards received from God's Word, our challenge is to avoid arrogance. Becoming prideful of our standards can have the inadvertent side effect of us thinking more highly of ourselves than we ought to think.

Here are a few ideas to help us retain humility as we engage those who believe differently or even have no belief at all.

Be willing to acknowledge truth where it is found. In our day, many conservative Christians have bought the political ruminations of talk radio and believe that "incrementalism" is the worst enemy. As a result, many such people brush aside anything spoken or written by one with whom they disagree, lest that political or theological opponent appear to gain an upper hand. Jesus did not do this. In fact, he was quick to affirm when and where his opponents were right, even as he spoke to their errors. If we really want to make an impact on people's lives, we should be willing to learn from them what we can while openly admitting that our own knowledge is limited. The Scriptures are inerrant, but we aren't.

Learn to recognize unbelievers first *as people loved by God.* Does "God so loved the world" only apply to people who are like us or people whom we like? We must remember that all people who choose to reject Christ are still loved by God. Who are we to pick and choose the persons we will love? When we recognize unbelievers first as people God loves, it will be easier for our love to follow.

Learn to recognize unbelievers as victims of the enemy. The Scriptures say that all unbelievers are under the deception of the wicked one. They are not the enemy; their souls are enslaved to sin and held captive by the enemy. They have the same need to be rescued as we had before our own salvation through Jesus Christ.

Intentionally befriend an unbeliever who is "out there." People are not projects; they retain a marred version of the image of God and desperately need to be restored to the wholeness of life in Christ. When Jesus saw Zacchaeus in the tree, he did not say, "Well, well, well, what have we here? A rebellious, God-hating tax collector!" On the contrary, he invited himself to Zacchaeus's house for dinner and a conversation. With Zacchaeus, Jesus was willing to push beyond the surface of obvious differences to his actual point of need. It is a place that Zacchaeus might have ignored or not even known existed, but it is a place that can be uncovered by a friend.

Commit to befriend and genuinely love people even when they do not come to faith in Christ. This is not to say we stop sharing the gospel but that we remain faithful friends even if others are resistant to it. If we predicate our friendships simply on "an opportunity to lead them to Christ" without a passionate commitment to the relationship itself, we will come across as disingenuous and may even turn them away from the faith we declare.

It is not without reason that Jesus said, "God did not send his Son into the world to condemn the world, but to save the world through him" (John 3:17). It lends power to the description of Jesus as "a friend of sinners."

Infiltrating culture with the gospel is the first priority in the context of mission. Those who live in the West will move forward when we relegate the culture wars to the back burner in favor of living out the love of Christ.

Dr. Ed Stetzer

Ed is president of LifeWay Research and LifeWay's missiologist in residence. He has planted, revitalized, and pastored churches; trained pastors and church planters on five continents; and written dozens of articles and books, including *Compelled by Love* and *Lost and Found.* Find Ed at *www.edstetzer.com.*

Chapter 10

THE MOSQUE NEXT DOOR

Building Relationships with the Religious

People who are not interested in something in general are rarely interested in a new version of it. It's like trying to get a non-coffee drinker like myself to try a Sumatran blend instead of the Colombian blend. I don't like *any* coffee. You could pour an entire bag of sugar and a gallon of milk into a grande cup, and I still won't like it. It's the same principle with starting a church. How can you get people excited about something that does not yet exist, especially if they don't like church to begin with? Starting a church in Seattle, one of the most unchurched cities in the United States, is even more difficult. Starting a youth group in a church in Seattle complicates matters even more.

By the time we had arrived in Seattle to work with the new church plant, a talented team filled with phenomenal leaders, singers, Bible teachers, lawyers, and even a state legislator was hard at work to get The Anchor Baptist Church (aka "The Anchor) started. When I discovered that our friend who had invited us to join this church-planting adventure had been telling his core team how effective he knew we would be in reaching students, I began feeling nervous.

The team of volunteers we were asked to lead had big hearts. We planned and dreamed and schemed about ways to attract teenagers to our brand-new youth group. The seven of us created a remarkable plan: we were going to transform the teens of Seattle with "Youth Explosion '94," a bold mixture of water balloons, dodgeball, loud music, free food, giveaways, and general bedlam. We planned to have the event in our parking lot, knowing that as other teens walked by and saw the crowd, they would be unable to resist the desire to join us. With snazzy flyers in hand, we visited the local high schools, video game arcades, malls, and parks.

Opening night arrived, and the seven of us were ready. Our planning and hard work were about to pay huge dividends. We couldn't wait to kick off this brand-new youth ministry. Seattle would never be the same. *We* would never be the same. People would soon be clamoring for the books we would be writing, which would describe our successful efforts in reaching so many unchurched teens. This was the moment for which we had been praying, dreaming, planning, and preparing. This was our moment! How many dozens or even hundreds of kids could we expect?

We were ready.

No one came.

Unfortunately, the youth of Seattle did not share our enthusiasm —not even the one kid who already went to our church. That night there were seven adults and *zero* teens. I tried to maintain a calm facade. All great leaders fail at one time or another. They become great as a result of their response to failure. They do not give up when things become difficult. When failure stares them in the face, they refuse to blink.

Rallying our team together, I assumed that the teens, who really *had* wanted to come, just did not have transportation. Our new plan: a few of us would drive back to some of the sites we had canvassed earlier in the week to pick up the kids and take them to the church parking lot.

As I was driving to a local high school, I began to ponder the situation. What had happened? Teenagers in Texas would show up to events I created. I had read books about how to reach others and how to grow youth groups. I had even attended a Purpose Driven Church conference. How could I have failed so miserably? If Debbie hadn't been waiting for me back at the parking lot, I may have just kept driving all the way back to Texas. But then a sense of urgency seeped into my mind: I had to find a teenager to take back with me — any teenager. I could not go back without one.

Driving down 35th Avenue, I saw my salvation. I saw a young guy playing basketball all by himself at the high school's outdoor courts. Confidence began to mix with my feelings of urgency. This young guy was going to come to our event and love it! I was going to be so persuasive he would not be able to turn me down. In fact, I was not going to take no for an answer.

I circled around the school, keeping him in sight as I considered what I would say. When I finally stopped, I saw that he had noticed me. This was going to be easy! I had already caught his attention with my sweet ride, my 1989 Chevrolet Cavalier. "Teenagers always look up to people with cars," I thought. Now I wouldn't have to come up with some nifty way to start the conversation.

"How ya doing?" I asked.

"OK," he responded.

For some reason, he seemed somewhat nervous. "He must be shy," I thought. He had very dark skin and a well-kept Afro, not a particularly popular look among African-American kids at the time. (Most preferred the bald head of Michael Jordan or the cornrows of Allen Iverson.) He appeared to be about fourteen years old.

I jumped right into my spiel: "You don't want to miss the greatest youth event of the summer. Just up the hill, we're having "Youth Explosion '94." Ever heard of it?"

"What?" He was slowly backing away from me.

I reached out for his bicycle and continued. "We can put your bicycle in the trunk of my car so you don't have to ride up the hill." I noticed he was holding the basketball tightly and inching farther away from me.

"Don't worry, we'll be done by eight thirty so you can get home before dark. Sound good?" I assumed that his apprehension in going with me may have been related to some sort of curfew.

I picked up his bicycle and started carrying it to my car. Looking back, I was surprised to see that he hadn't begun to follow me to my car. "Come on," I assured him. "You're going to love it!"

He seemed reluctant as he slowly began walking toward the car. Putting his bicycle into the trunk, I opened the passenger door. Boy, this guy was really quiet and shy. "Come on. Get in! I guarantee you're going to love it, or your money back." I loved that joke. Youth Explosion '94 was free! I was surprised he didn't laugh.

After a little more coaxing and convincing, I finally got him to get in the car. As we started driving up the hill, I introduced myself to him and asked him his name.

"What?" His eyes seemed to be especially wide open. I began to wonder if he had some sort of hearing deficiency, so I began speaking louder.

I pointed to myself as I half shouted, "My name is Eric. What's your name?"

He seemed to hear me this time, but he didn't smile the way most people do when they finally understand what is being asked.

He answered back with a thick accent, "My name is Seid Abdu." Seid was not shy or deaf. He was fourteen years old, and he was from Eritrea, a country in northern East Africa. Getting picked up in a car by a stranger to go to a church was a new experience, for Seid, I later discovered, was a Muslim.

When we arrived back at The Anchor, I discovered that another teenager had come with her dad. Even though two teens are more than one, I felt completely discouraged. We had tried so hard to create a ministry, a program, an event, that students would enjoy attending and that they'd want to bring their friends to. The two teens who did come seemed to enjoy themselves, but the fact was, only those two teens were there.

That night was a turning point for me. Not only did my way of doing ministry change — from a more program-oriented approach to a more relational one — but Seid became a friend as well. Seid attended the mosque on Fridays, and he began coming to our youth group on Wednesdays. So often I had viewed ministry through the lens of "strategies," and subconsciously I had viewed people as projects. When I thought about people from other religious backgrounds, I tried to come up with ways to prove to them why their beliefs were wrong and mine were right. After using this method with Seid, I realized I was hurting our relationship and risking our friendship for the sake of debate. Befriending Seid helped me move from program evangelism to friendship evangelism — becoming a friend of someone who had a different perspective on the world.

Interestingly, Seid ended up inviting more people to our youth group than anyone else over the next several years, and many of his friends moved closer to Christ. As I got to know Seid, I discovered that the key to helping a Muslim, Buddhist, Hindu, Catholic, Baptist, Lutheran, or anyone for that matter begin a relationship with Christ involves developing a genuine friendship with him or her.

Just before Debbie and I moved from Seattle to Los Angeles, I asked Seid why he got into the car the first time we met on the basketball courts. A smile crossed his lips as he answered, "I didn't think I had a choice. I thought you were kidnapping me."

PROXIMITY EQUALS OPPORTUNITY

In our world, religions abound. In our desperate search for meaning, we cling to anything that helps us make sense of things. So many people have never heard that Jesus came to free us from our brokenness and from religion. For those who have heard the name "Jesus," so many of them do not know the full story. As we interact with a pluralistic world, rather than trying to convert others to our beliefs, we need to look for opportunities to share the life-transforming, heart-changing message of Christ with those who want to hear. Through our relationships, our actions, and our conversations, we need to learn how to create a genuine interest within others.

Most people have needs that create within them an openness toward God. If we can listen and ask enough questions, we can help people see that God loves and cares for them and offers a life filled with adventure. Looking for those who are already open parallels Jesus' style as he sent the disciples out to look for persons who loved peace (see Luke 10:6).

With the world moving into our neighborhoods, we cannot assume that inviting people to church will change their lives. Too often our churches remain less than impressive, and those we invite initially need a reason to decide to go. Getting involved in someone's life allows us to share our lives honestly with them in a way that gives hope when they feel hopeless. When a friend sees us go through trials while relying on God and our friendships, they are more likely to seek us out when they are struggling. Proximity allows us opportunity for significant conversations.

In our Seattle days, a mission group once came to town to perform a concert in one of the local parks. I had a chance to meet Sovann, a young man who had grown up in Southeast Asia. Sovann seemed intrigued by our group. He agreed to join me for coffee, and we had a great conversation about his life. The conversation naturally moved toward God as I asked him to tell me about his spiritual journey. He shared about his childhood in Southeast Asia, his move to the United States, and his awareness of God but his inability to know for sure whether God was real. Soon he was listening to my story as well. After sharing with him about how following Jesus had completely changed my life, I asked if he would be interested in connecting to God personally. With a completely serious look on his face, he looked me right in the eye as he said, "I want to, but the voices won't let me."

In conversations with those who follow other religions or who simply abandoned Christianity, I've generally found that most people need a life of meaning, significance, adventure, peace, and hope. "The removal of voices" had not cracked the top ten list of reasons why people wanted to connect to God. Within the next few months, Sovann chose to follow Christ, in spite of the voices and his Buddhist background. He continued taking his medication for schizophrenia, which seemed to help a bit, but Sovann truly found healing as he served others and began to ignore the voices. Treating the voices as a temptation such as worry or lust, he took captive every thought (see 2 Corinthians 10:5) and prayed to God whenever the voices got loud. He replaced the voices with Scriptures he had memorized. He replaced the behaviors he struggled with when lonely by investing in the lives of others. The last I heard from Sovann, he was a youth leader in a church, serving God and no longer taking medication for strange voices.

We need more missionaries in our cities. The term "missionary" should describe all those who follow Christ. At Mosaic, the dozens of families and adults we have commissioned to serve in other countries are considered our "overseas workers" or "international leaders" rather than our "missionaries." We have not abdicated the responsibility for helping others find peace with God to just those who move overseas. Along with them, *we* are missionaries as well — our mission field just happens to be Los Angeles.

For people who have served as missionaries to Los Angeles, moving overseas becomes an easy adjustment. They have developed the skills necessary for effective ministry — catalyzing relationships with new people and helping those who want to know God to discover how. At one point just a few years ago, we sent on average one adult per month into the most unchurched parts of the world. More recently, after the devastating tsunami that hit southeast Asia, we sent eighteen people to go to one of the more devastated countries to help with relief work. Working alongside the four families from our church who have been living there long-term, we have since had three young adults and a family of four choose to move to this country indefinitely. Meeting the needs of people in this devastated part of the world allows these men, women, and kids to show Christ's love for those who are hurting. As time goes on, our desire is that people will discover Jesus for themselves through the lives of those who are there representing him.

For those who do not live overseas full-time, we have created opportunities to engage the world here in LA, as well as to participate in short-term projects around the globe. As we utilize relief projects, films, music, church planting, leadership training, and other resources, we are actively creating the future by developing friendships with people who are spiritual seekers all across the globe.

AN ANCIENT MYSTERY REVEALED

"What is the secret?"

Fatima, a woman from North Africa, had just fasted for an entire month. She was obeying the stipulations of Ramadan, one of the year's holiest times for a Muslim. She earnestly sought to do everything she could to make her life right with God, yet something was still missing.

"What secret?"

After months of getting to know Fatima in North Africa, Nancy, an American, was excited. Could this be the moment for which she had been preparing and praying? The two women had met after their daughters had become friends at their neighborhood school. Nancy and her husband had moved from the Midwest of the United States to North Africa to start a business. Their goal was not financial but spiritual. They were there with their four children to share this secret with all of the people who wanted to hear about it.

Fatima whispered, "What is the secret of Christmas?"

Nancy smiled and began revealing the "secret," which Fatima had never heard before. Fatima eagerly took the book Nancy offered — a book she promised would explain the "secret."

This is a great example of how we Christians need to get close to others so they can see how real and powerful our God is, especially as we allow him to transform our lives. We need to reframe the conversation. We act as though our God can beat up other gods, yet even Jesus rejected this approach. It isn't a question of Christianity's being the best "religion." Rather than starting a religion, Jesus invaded history with a secret.

With people all over the world clamoring for the attention of God or the gods, Jesus approached his mission with clarity for those who had listening ears. Revealing the secret remained dangerous, but Jesus would not die before the appointed time. As a result of the danger, Jesus' message was often delivered in parables and metaphors, such as the well-known stories of the prodigal son and the good Samaritan. These parables left many in the audience perplexed, for only those who wanted to hear the truth could do so.

Even so, Jesus revealed only enough for people to begin their journey with him, leaving much more to be discovered. Even when someone responded to Jesus' invitation to follow him, that person usually had no idea where he or she would end up going. During Jesus' ministry, many walked away once they decided that Jesus was not who they had hoped he was, leaving only about 120 people who considered themselves to be followers of Jesus immediately after Jesus' death on a cross. Most people failed to understand the secret he was revealing. Others heard Jesus' message and rejected him because of its implications. Jesus revealed a mystery that had long been sought by prophets and the righteous, yet many did not understand what he was saying. What was this secret that Jesus finally revealed?

In Matthew's gospel we find this:

Then [Jesus] told them many things in parables, saying: ...
"Whoever has ears, let them hear."

The disciples came to him and asked, "Why do you speak
to the people in parables?"

He replied, "The knowledge of the secrets of the kingdom
of heaven has been given to you, but not to them. Those who
have will be given more, and they will have an abundance. As
for those who do not have, even what they have will be taken
from them. This is why I speak to them in parables:

"Though seeing, they do not see;
    though hearing, they do not hear or understand....

"But blessed are your eyes because they see, and your ears
because they hear. Truly I tell you, many prophets and righteous people longed to see what you see but did not see it, and
to hear what you hear but did not hear it."

Matthew 13:3, 9 – 13, 16

What is this secret? Jesus waited for thirty years to begin his
public ministry in order to care for his family as a carpenter. After
all that time, Jesus' first message was simply, "Repent, for the kingdom of heaven has come near" (Matthew 4:17).

The kingdom is almost here!

But soon his message shifted. The kingdom was no longer near;
it was actually here. After Jesus began healing the sick, driving out
demons, and proclaiming the message of the kingdom, people began
to see the winds of something new. Jesus was performing signs and
miracles, clarifying to the world his role as the Messiah.

When Jesus began speaking in parables in order to disguise his message, he spoke about this new kingdom. Repeatedly Jesus used the words "the kingdom of heaven is like ..." (Matthew 13:31, 33, 44, 45, 47, and so on). Jesus was describing a kingdom that no one had ever seen or experienced. His kingdom was very different from any other kingdom. Rather than being advanced through war and conflict, Jesus' kingdom is advanced through peace and love.

Jesus' secret was revealed. Jesus had come to establish a kingdom filled with men, women, and children from every tribe, language, people, and nation (Revelation 5:9). This kingdom is filled with Jews, Hindus, Buddhists, Muslims, and Christians who are now for Jesus.

Jesus revealed a new kingdom. He hadn't come as a political messiah; nor had he come to start a better religion. Jesus brought the eternal into the present. Rather than freeing political prisoners and establishing his reign through an earthly political or geographical model, Jesus came to start a spiritual kingdom whose citizens would come from all of the nations and out of all of the religions. To enter this kingdom, we need to step out of the temporal world and enter the eternal world through faith by asking Christ to become our King, no matter who we are or from where we come. Those who surrender their lives to become God's servants join him in his mission to rescue others who remain unaware of the freedom this invisible kingdom brings.

You may be thinking, "This isn't a secret! I know about this kingdom. Everyone does." *You* may have heard about God's kingdom, but so many others have not experienced it. So many others have never stepped into eternity while their feet are planted on the ground. So many others are stuck trying to find what some of us see so clearly.

Several months ago, my wife, Debbie, and I met a young woman from the Middle East who is living in LA. The woman went to see the movie *The Da Vinci Code* merely to be entertained. Instead, she had nightmares after she went to bed that night. For some reason, she felt haunted by Jesus and couldn't discern the meaning of her dreams. Looking for answers, she visited our westside gathering, a place she had come once before on a whim months earlier. Her first question to one of our greeters after the gathering betrayed her insecurities: "Am I welcome here since I am Muslim?" She was assured not only that she was welcome but also that Jesus loved her. As the conversation progressed, she chose to trust Jesus, even though she knew so little about him. What she did know was that she needed love and forgiveness and hope.

During lunch with Debbie, me, and our kids that same day, she asked what she was supposed to do so that God would love her. Debbie insisted that she didn't have to do anything for God to love her but that she was already loved by God. Instead, her own growing love for God would be the motivation for the changes she would soon want to make. Overwhelmed by this unconditional love, tears filled her eyes several times. I encouraged her to begin to listen to God's voice through the Scriptures, the whispered thoughts in her mind, the messages she heard on Sundays, the conversations she had with others, and even the most mundane things she saw and experienced during each day. I told her that God is actively pursuing her and showing his love. I mentioned that God could even speak to her through the fortune cookie she had sitting in front of her. She quickly began to open the cookie — a response I didn't expect — and I began to pray that the message didn't say something like, "You like Chinese food."

After reading her fortune, she looked at Debbie and began to sob again. God *had* spoken to her through the fortune cookie, which read, "There is a true and sincere friendship between you both."

Whether she saw this as a true and sincere friendship between her and God or between her and Debbie — or both — I'm not sure. A moment later, Caleb handed her his fortune as well, which read, "You are heading in the right direction."

When we understand this revelation from Christ, everything changes. We cannot see our relationship with God as simply our ticket into heaven. When we enter a relationship with God, we become citizens of a new kingdom. Our calling in life is to serve the King by serving others outside of this kingdom. We must infiltrate earthly kingdoms by guiding others to switch their loyalty to Christ's invisible kingdom. Stepping into the invisible kingdom reveals our destiny. We discover who we are meant to be and what we are meant to do.

THE RELIGIOUS WRONG

Religion requires action. Religious people often perform rituals to try to gain access to God or to gain some sort of spiritual edge. Throughout the world, people intrinsically feel disconnected from God. We know we are sinful. We know we are unworthy. Sadly, as a result, we submit ourselves to the rules and regulations of religion in the hope that it will help — for some it is animal sacrifice; for others it is attending church, giving money, forsaking some things, doing other things. The motivation for doing these things is to get closer to God.

Jesus' message, however, was very different. He taught that the practice of "religion" cannot be the answer. We can never do enough to reach God. We are incapable of doing enough good to come to God on our own merits (see Mark 10:17 – 31). God is perfect; we are imperfect. Rather than prescribing a "do" and "don't" list, Jesus calls us to lose our lives and begin a relationship with him on his terms (see Mark 8:34 – 38). We cannot negotiate or work our way into his presence. We acknowledge that our efforts are meaningless. We need God's forgiveness offered through Jesus' death on the cross. We need his leadership in our lives, which is possible because he rose from the dead and offers his Spirit to all who follow him.

I am not a fan of horror movies. I don't like them, and I never recommend them. I was once invited to attend a screening for the movie *Constantine*, starring Keanu Reeves. I was told it was like *The Matrix* with an even more spiritual edge to it. After the first two minutes, my wife had closed her eyes. Two minutes later, she left the theater. It was more like *The Exorcist* than like *The Matrix*. The images of demons and hell were horrifying. I stayed to watch the movie for one reason: John Constantine was trying to earn his way into heaven by casting demons into hell. The marketing blitz included the phrase "Hell wants him; heaven won't take him; the earth needs him." I thought it was fascinating that the creators of this movie realized that even casting demons out of little girls was not good enough to earn the right to enter heaven. None of us can enter God's presence as the direct result of our works (see Ephesians 2:8 – 9). We need grace. We need forgiveness. We need God. We cannot depend on adherence to religion or good works.

As Jesus communicated his message in parables, he was showing a new way out of religion and into a relationship with God. He infuriated the religious leaders to the point that they arrested him and eventually had him handed over to the Romans to be crucified. The religious leaders did not like Jesus' message. He was offering a new life that could be found through a relationship rather than through following rules. The religious leaders were able to control others through their regulations and policies. They knew that if people began to follow Jesus, they would stop obeying them. They would lose their prestige, their power, and even their funding. They manipulated others based on their ability to instill fear. They had convinced many sincere people that if they did not practice their religion, they would lose their spiritual hope. In contrast, Jesus himself claimed to be the very source of hope.

Jesus was willing to die to make his point: religion does not work because religion is humanity's attempt to earn God's favor. Jesus proclaims through his death and his words, "I am the way and the truth and the life. No one comes to the Father except through me" (John 14:6). Jesus spoke in parables so that he might continue to spread his message while the religious listened without really hearing him. The religious did not get him. They still don't.

If you interact with people who do not follow Jesus, I'm sure you have heard the statement, "I find Jesus to be a compelling person and his message to be inspiring, but what about all of the other religions? How can Jesus claim to be the *only* way to God?" People seem to like and even respect Jesus, no matter where they come from and no matter what their spiritual journey may have been. Jesus is one of the coolest people ever to have lived, according to just about everyone. The one thing people do *not* like about him is his claim to be the *only* way to God.

Jesus' claim is unique. Jesus is the only one who died for the sins of others. Jesus does not offer practices or disciplines that will ensure communion with God. He is God. Jesus did not come to start a religion; he came to start a revolution. Sadly, some of us have turned his revolution into an institution.

An actor who had had small parts in major productions once came to our church. Frustrated, he wrote a note on the back of a guest card, voicing his displeasure with how intolerant we seemed to be. Without signing his name, he left his phone number, so I called him. I wanted to discover the roots of his frustration. Over the phone he explained that he had heard that we were a diverse community, so he was surprised to find out that we weren't. Puzzled, I explained that we have people from many different nationalities within our community and that we have people attending Mosaic who come from different religious backgrounds and who practice different lifestyles. We are open to those who are spiritually seeking. He responded, "Well, it has become obvious to me that you believe that Jesus is God and that he is the only way to salvation."

He had me there. In that sense, we aren't diverse. We believe that Jesus is God and that he is the one true source of hope for the entire world. Because we have discovered the life-changing power of a relationship with Jesus, we want everyone to know what we have found. We have found life, and this life is for every person — people from every nation and from every religion. Life is freely offered to anyone desiring to find it.

Even after we choose to follow Jesus, recognizing that we have been saved by grace through faith, too often we start to live our lives for him out of obligation. Just as we were saved by grace through faith (Ephesians 2:8 – 9), we need to *live* by grace through faith (Colossians 2:6 – 7). We need to allow God to transform our passions so that we do the right things out of gratitude rather than out of greed. We do the right things as a way of thanking him for all he has given us rather than doing the right things because we expect to get something in return. Do you want to discover the secret? Enter the relationship, and shed the religion.

Having lunch with this actor sometime later, I was surprised that he hadn't felt excluded by the fact that he was gay and had lived with his partner for twelve years. No, he insisted, he felt welcomed, but he had come to know that our goal was to have him connect to Jesus personally. He had discovered our secret.

SPECTATOR SLOWING

Living in Los Angeles has turned me into a stargazer. Everywhere I go, I look for someone famous. I'm not exactly sure why I do. I never say anything to them. I have considered coming up with a phrase to say to the famous people I meet just to hear their response. I've considered approaching a celebrity and saying, "Excuse me, do you know what time it is?" I would love to see their facial expression after being asked such a mundane question. I promise I'm not a stalker; I'm just a collector.

In the last few years I have seen many different celebrities, but I've actually talked with only one person. I just couldn't resist starting a conversation as I sat next to Richard Jefferson of the New Jersey Nets. I am a huge basketball fan. As a short white guy, I wish I enjoyed horse racing or gymnastics. Those are the two sports I could have pursued professionally. Instead, I have to love the sport I had the least amount of hope to pursue once I survived junior high. When I saw Richard Jefferson, I had to say hello. He was on my fantasy basketball team. I was sitting right next to him, and we talked for just a few minutes — until he glanced at his boarding pass and discovered that he was at the wrong gate. I thought it was quite a clever way to end our conversation until I spotted him later getting on a plane at another gate. He had not left our conversation because he wanted to do so; he left because he actually had to go catch the right flight. I realized that he wasn't trying to get away from me after all. Richard Jefferson was now my friend!

I know I only had one conversation with him, but from then on, when I saw him on TV playing basketball, I would call out to my wife, "Debbie, my friend is on TV!" When watching the NBA with my family or friends, I would point out how well "my friend" was shooting, dunking, scoring, and defending. After just one conversation, I considered myself to be someone who *knows* Richard Jefferson.

Now, before you ask if Richard Jefferson has placed a restraining order on me, let me pose a question: Have we done a similar thing with Jesus? We've seen him do amazing things around us. We may have even had a remarkable conversation with him at some point in our life. As a result, whenever someone mentions his name, we are quick to point out that we know him. Do we *really* know him? Or do we simply know all about him?

Jesus no longer wanted the spectators to slow down his movement on earth. Jesus was followed by the peasants rather than the paparazzi. If they could have taken pictures of him, they would have. Jesus' fame had spread throughout the Middle East. Huge crowds wanted to see him, even if it was from a distance. Jesus was hot.

Even today people treat Jesus like a celebrity. In the past few years, we've had "Jesus fashion" with "WWJD" bracelets and "Jesus is my homeboy" hats and shirts. We all know who he is. We all have stories to tell about him. We all hope to meet him so we can tell others about the encounter, but do we really know him?

Jesus has all the fame he wants. More than fame, Jesus desires followers. While walking this earth, he would often say things to scare away those who were not serious about making a commitment to him and to his leadership in their lives. He wanted to clarify that he was not simply on earth to offer a free medical clinic. He was ultimately here to do something more extraordinary than teach great truths, heal diseases, and raise the dead. He was here to perform the greatest miracle of all — to transform lives.

As Jesus' life was coming to an end, there was a man who encountered Jesus' ability to forgive, yet he was not freed from his physical affliction. Two men were crucified at the same time Jesus hung from a cross. One man hurled insults at Jesus: "Aren't you the Messiah? Save yourself and us!" (Luke 23:39). The other criminal rebuked the man, saying, "Don't you fear God ... since you are under the same sentence? We are punished justly, for we are getting what our deeds deserve. But this man has done nothing wrong" (Luke 23:40 – 41). This man's faith was not based on what Jesus could do for him. He didn't require a miracle to believe in Jesus. The other criminal was demanding to be rescued. This criminal was acknowledging that he deserved to be punished for his sinful actions — and he was then able to experience the greatest miracle known to humanity. He was able to see what the other criminal could not see — the secret that Jesus had revealed.

He turned to Jesus and said, "Jesus, remember me when you come into your kingdom." Jesus' response echoes down through the ages: "Truly I tell you, today you will be with me in paradise" (Luke 23:42 – 43). The criminal had moved from being a spectator to a genuine follower. He was no longer interested in what Jesus could offer him in the present. He was more concerned with stepping into Jesus' kingdom.

The disciples thought they had discovered Christ's secret. They were able to drive out demons and perform miracles in Christ's name! Not only were they witnesses to his miraculous acts; they were now in on the action. Jesus had sent seventy-two of his followers out to change the world. They returned excited about the extraordinary experiences they had during their adventure:

> The seventy-two returned with joy and said, "Lord, even the demons submit to us in your name."

> He [Jesus] replied, "I saw Satan fall like lightning from heaven. I have given you authority to trample on snakes and scorpions and to overcome all the power of the enemy; nothing will harm you. However, do not rejoice that the spirits submit to you, but rejoice that your names are written in heaven."
>
> **Luke 10:17 – 20**

What Jesus did on earth was miraculous. What Jesus enables others to do in his name is remarkable. What is more impressive than all of these earthly miracles? Jesus can transform us eternally.

The religious are looking for ways to reach God through their own actions and merit. The spectators are looking for what Jesus can do for them. The committed are willing to let Jesus have their entire lives, no matter what may happen.

A friend of mine decided to follow Jesus so that he could help others who were even further away from God than he was. A few months later, someone brought up the idea of heaven. He laughed off the concept until we insisted that heaven is real and that *he* is going to be there. He had chosen to live for Jesus regardless of what happened to him after he died.

We need to help others follow Jesus for what he has already done for them and for what he has prepared for them to do rather than for what they get from him, and we need to do the same.

FIELD NOTES

"Please tell me how you raise your children," Shamira said as she sat across from me in Starbucks.

I never thought I'd share the gospel with a Muslim, but as we sipped our drinks, I explained our family's relationship with Jesus, the power of the Holy Spirit, and our reliance on God. This opportunity didn't come quickly.

Two years earlier, our daughters, Erin and Zenna, became friends at school. This friendship didn't even hit my radar until Erin changed her lunch choices so as not to offend her kosher friend.

Eventually, Zenna and her brother would occasionally come to my home after school. One day, when she picked them up, Shamira was really sick. I asked if I could pray for her. I prayed a simple prayer — that God would heal her from the top of her head to the bottom of her feet — in Jesus name. She was healed that night. She was so excited that she stopped by the next day just to tell me.

When Shamira first invited me to tea, I was intimidated. She worked in the medical field and lived a kosher lifestyle. Her house was spotless. I thought she would be turned off by my obvious unkosher and rather messy way of life. Instead, she kept coming back for prayer.

Then we moved to another town, and my kids changed schools. Surely this would be the end of our friendship, I thought. Instead, about six months later, Shamira asked me to tea, which is when we met at Starbucks.

Apparently, when Erin left school, the dynamics of her friend group changed dramatically. Shamira could tell that our family made a differ-ence. She wanted to know why. In a few short sentences, I explained the freedom we walk in because of Jesus. "We don't teach our kids to live by rules but to listen to God and do what he says. We believe that Jesus died on the cross so that we can have a relationship with God and know him personally. When we accept his gift, we are able to live a life in which we walk as the people God intended us to be."

Honestly, I thought she was going to think I was a freak. So, instead of trying to be as literate as possible, I just tried to be as honest as possible. I told her how our kids were able to walk in love because we prayed that they would see others the way God sees them.

Instead of being freaked-out, Shamira began to share some of her hopes, concerns, and dreams with me, and always we would pray. Once, she came into the church where I was working to find me. Recently, she even brought her father over, and we shared tea.

The most surprising thing about this friendship is how I have grown. God is teaching me gentleness by showing me an example in Shamira. He is also challenging and coaching me in the area of hospitality. Isn't it amazing how God can bring about growth in us while using us to draw others to himself?

Do you want to love Muslims or others from different religious backgrounds but don't know how? Here are some action ideas:

- Ask God to show you the Muslims, Buddhists, Taoists, and so forth that he has already put in your life.

- Look for opportunities to deepen those relationships. Get to know them. Right after 9/11, I asked a Muslim lady who lived on my street how she was doing. She told me that work was hard for her because everyone thought she was the enemy. I let her know I would be a friend and that I would pray. We talked every few weeks for the next year or two.

- Solidify these relationships by being a friend. Invite people into your life. Be real. Be honest. Find things you have in common, and develop friendships based on them.

- When you go to the store, intentionally check out with the same clerk every time. Pray for her by name daily. When you see her, ask her how she's doing. When she shares about some problem, offer to pray — then check back and find out how God answered your prayer.

Kim Martinez

Kim lives in the Seattle area with her husband and four kids. Her passion is to help her kids and other people discover and become what God created them to be. Kim has been a pastor, writer, and an administrative professional. She lives to see what new adventure God has around the corner. You can find Kim online at *www.kimmartinezstayingfocused.wordpress.com.*

■ Conclusion

APATHETICS ANONYMOUS

Activating Personal Change

During my sophomore year at Baylor University, I served as a co-chairman of the Revival Steering Committee. I was passionate about seeing spiritual change take place at my Christian school. So many people had grown indifferent to Christ, had walked away from their faith, or had never even begun a relationship with God. The need for a change could not have been any more obvious than in the cafeteria on any given Sunday afternoon. Guys who had passed out from their Saturday night exploits would struggle to get up by noon so they could dress for lunch — to make it appear that they had just arrived from church. Why would they go to so much trouble? Were their parents in the cafeteria? Was there a girl in there they were trying to impress? Usually they went to such great lengths to hide the effects of throwing back a few brews so that they might maintain their appearance of being deeply religious. They were giving in to the peer pressure for the sake of appearing as though they were devoted to God.

As you can probably discern, as students at a Christian college, we were not known for our authenticity.

For months our committee had prayed and planned together. We had worked out all of the logistics. We had chosen a speaker, a worship band, and a concert headliner. We came up with a plan for marketing, for working with the facilities managers and faculty members, and for follow-up. One of the most difficult challenges had to do with choosing a theme. We wanted to set the tone for the event — plus we needed something cool to put on the T-shirts. As hip and inventive college students, we finally settled on "Life Is a Compromise ... Not!" You may laugh now, but back in 1991, that phrase was bad (as in "really good"). OK, I know it's ridiculous, but would it help you appreciate it more to know that "Life Is a Compromise" was on the front and "Not!" was on the back?

Have you ever been so excited for something that there was no way it could ever turn out as good as you hoped it would? In my case, what I hope for usually never quite happens, but neither does what I fear. But at twenty years of age, I experienced one of the most significant events of my life — yet it took place in the most unexpected way.

Once the week finally arrived, our revival was remarkable. For four nights, our best efforts had been rewarded with an incredible experience. Louie Giglio and his "Choice" praise team led the music. Dave Busby, a dynamic speaker and a walking miracle, spoke each night. My co-chairman, Frances, and I were responsible to make the announcements. Everything was coming together just as we hoped, until the night came when we had invited all of our parents and the faculty members to attend. Suddenly our script was no longer being followed, and our plan began to unravel.

With great effort, Dave Busby challenged us each night. He had cystic fibrosis, a disease that caused difficulty in breathing (at the time he was one of the oldest people in the world with the disease). After speaking to a crowd of thousands of college students, Busby required help to get back to his hotel room so he could clear his lungs from the excessive buildup of mucus. His passion and intensity really seemed to move the crowd, almost resulting in his death in the process.

On Thursday night, rather than issue an altar call, Dave Busby had something else in mind. Reading from Matthew 20:29 – 34, he compared us to the two blind men who shouted out to Jesus, pleading with him to help them and to heal them. "All of us have needs that only Jesus can meet," he declared, "but there are people all around you telling you to stop shouting out to Jesus. Tonight I want you to hear Jesus' words to the blind men as if he was directing them to you. Jesus is asking you, 'What do you want me to do for you?' What do you need from Jesus? There is a microphone here in the front. Right now, come and tell Jesus, in front of everyone else, what it is you need from him."

Our team of organizers sat stunned. What if no one came? Even worse, what if people did come to cry out to God on the microphone? What if someone said something profane or, God forbid, shared something personal or messy? Justin, one of the guys on our team who was sitting just a few chairs away from me, stood up. At first I assumed he was preparing to help those who might come forward since he was a part of the follow-up team. As he continued walking closer and closer to the microphone, I began to feel nauseous. He was about to speak, and he seemed to be crying. This was not going to be good. This was going to be completely embarrassing — not just for him but for me and the entire steering committee. We were supposed to have it all together. That's why we were the ones organizing revival!

Justin's hand shook as he reached for the microphone. He wiped away a tear from his cheek. Facing the stage rather than the crowd sitting behind him, he seemed to be oblivious to the thousands of eyes focused on him. With his voice trembling and the tears beginning to come faster than he could wipe them away, Justin sobbed into the microphone: "Jesus, I need you. I am so impure. I feel like I cannot stop having impure thoughts about the women I see on campus."

The young women on our team winced, suddenly feeling a bit underdressed in that moment. Unfortunately, Justin wasn't done exposing all of his struggles to Jesus — and since he was using the microphone to do so, to all of us as well. His eyes continued leaking moisture as his nose began running. If we didn't know how to specifically pray for Justin, he then gave us way more information than we wanted to hear.

If I had thought I felt uncomfortable before, this was unbearable. Groans of disgust and shock filled the auditorium as the crowd reacted to his honesty and emotion. Making the moment even that much more otherworldly, I was sitting next to my parents, who had driven down to see me make my announcements in front of all these people. I know they had not come to hear about Justin's secret shame.

Was this what Dave Busby had in mind?

As Justin walked away from the microphone, I was surprised to see others descending from the upper levels and others from the floor level, all making their way to the front. A woman cried out, asking God to help her overcome her eating disorder. A male student shouted at God because he was so angry about the death of a loved one. His rage turned into brokenness as he asked Jesus to forgive him for his anger and to help him move forward. For over an hour, students continued to cry out to God, asking for help and forgiveness and healing. We had not planned for revival to actually take place at this revival, but it was happening. Everything that was transpiring was completely out of our control.

The members of the faculty and some of the parents began to leave, choosing to skip the banquet that had been scheduled for after the meeting. They had experienced enough revival for the evening. Suddenly my mind shifted from worrying over the logistics of the banquet, the departure of faculty members, and the timing of the announcements. Out of nowhere, I was blindsided by a deep sense that *I* needed something from Jesus too. I fought this feeling, which continued to build inside of me. I tried to just tell Jesus what I needed from my seat. I didn't need to go the microphone. I could make things right with God on my own right there where I was. I mean, I had been making announcements all week. I was the leader of the Revival Steering Committee! How could I stand up in front of my peers — and my parents for that matter — and share my own secret shame?

The sense of urgency grew as person after person shared publicly on the microphone. The time came when, rather than having dozens in line, as had been the case earlier in the evening, there were only about three people waiting their turn. Without explanation to my parents, I stood up and walked toward the line. My parents had lasted longer than I would have imagined they would. Perhaps they stayed because of their shock or their desire to see God at work; or more realistically, they probably stayed since they had ridden with me to the event. Whatever the case, I couldn't let the fact that they were there keep me from honestly admitting to Jesus what I needed from him.

At first, no sound came out of my open mouth. I worked harder, fighting through my own tears and emotion to share my deepest need. The words came stumbling out of my mouth louder than I had imagined they would: "God, I desperately need you. I don't love people. I don't care about people who do not know you. All I care about is myself. Help me to love people, no matter who they are or what they do. Help me to love people the way you do."

At this point, I completely lost control of my emotions.

I had grown up in a traditional Southern Baptist church, where the people did not display emotions. Instead, we sang hymns. Clapping after someone sang a solo in our church wasn't even appropriate. Here I was in front of everyone, admitting how selfish and unloving I was. If I thought finding a date was hard before, I figured I was completely out of luck now.

My parents are great people, but the emotion of the moment was out of their normal realm of experience as well. As I sat down, sobbing and with my head in my hands, my dad gave me a very nice, quick pat on the back to let me know that he wasn't completely humiliated by my personal revelation.

I honestly don't know if we really did experience revival that night, since no long-term changes seemed to happen on campus. (Really, I don't even remember any short-term changes.) The one thing I knew for sure was that I would never be the same. Jesus had answered my prayer. The world looked different to me. Rather than seeing the world as a place in which I had to conform, conquer, or comply, I saw people. I saw people with genuine needs — needs that could only be met by a God who loved them. I realized that God actually wanted me to be a part of meeting those needs, and, even more miraculously, I actually wanted this to be the case. I caught a glimpse of how God must feel when he looks at the billions of people in this world. When God looks at those who do not love him, he sees hope, potential, possibilities, and uniqueness — and he feels love. Suddenly I saw and felt the same things. Rather than the anger or judgment I had felt toward the "hypocrites" on campus, I felt concern, sorrow, and even shame, for I realized that I, too, lived a duplicitous life.

This event seemed to be similar to Alcoholics Anonymous for me. Just by confessing that I was apathetic about others, I felt revitalized toward changing. Announcing my secret gave me the courage to move forward. God was changing my heart from apathy to action.

It wasn't as though I had never loved before, and it certainly wouldn't be true to say that I have loved others completely and unconditionally ever since. Instead, that night sent my life down a different path — one that followed a very different trajectory. I began making decisions as guided by God to serve, love, and influence people rather than thinking in terms of my ministry "career." Position, power, public presence, and even payment no longer seemed as important as people. After asking God to help me love people — especially people who did not love God or love me — he sent me out to find them. God changed my desires.

As followers of Christ, we need to actively pursue friendships with people we have tended to avoid. We need to see others with God's eyes and be willing to change how we live in order to serve and love those with whom we disagree or those we have even historically disliked. God sent others to us. Now it is our turn to be sent by him to others.

ACKNOWLEDGMENTS

I have always found the speeches at the Academy Awards annoying. The Oscar winners start thanking people whom I've never met; yet for some reason I still watch to see what might happen. Will Hilary Swank forget to thank her husband? Will Tom Hanks "out" his former drama teacher? Will the award winner cry, laugh, say something controversial or embarrassing, or even be forced off the stage by the music?

I know I haven't won any awards, but now, for the first time, I can empathize with the actors, directors, writers, and others who have trouble limiting their "thank you" list. I sincerely wish I could acknowledge each person's impact and how he or she contributed to this book and to this author, yet I sense a band waiting to begin belting out its tunes and rushing me away from this computer keyboard.

Having said all this, certain people have been instrumental in helping me with this project. First, I would like to thank my community — my family at Mosaic. I honestly feel I'm experiencing a glimpse of the early church. Debbie, Caleb, Trevi, and I have experienced love and authenticity in our friendships with the people who are Mosaic. Through great times and tragic times — and all of the other days in between — our community has helped remind us of who God has created us to be as individuals and as a body. It is a privilege to be a part of a team that strives to change the world and create the future.

I am forever indebted to Erwin and Kim McManus. Their leadership, creativity, character, and love for God and people have guided us to become who we are. They continue to challenge us to become people who are courageous, wise, and generous through the most powerful form of communication — the way they live their lives. Erwin continues to open doors for many of us, allowing us to run through them and find blessings on the other side. Without what I've learned from him, this book would never have existed. I am extremely grateful for his leadership, guidance, and friendship in my life.

I am grateful to Dana Elliott, Dana Evans, and Sueann Cho for reading, editing, and creating time for me to work on this project. I am grateful for Steve Saccone, Jason Jaggard, David Arcos, Jimmy Duke, Janice Sakuma, Jaime Puente, Greg SooHoo, Robert Martinez, Enrique Vasquez, Rick Yamamoto, Monique Smith, Chad Becker, Dave Auda, Neil Nakamoto, Eileen Lu, Marcus "Goodie" Goodloe, Joby Harris, Rickey Williams, Ralph Neighbor III, Scott Long, Alex and Adriana McManus, the paid staff, the volunteer staff, the protégés, the interns, and the community at Mosaic — all of whom have contributed their eyes for editing, their stories for inspiration, and their friendship for encouragement. I am so blessed to have each of you in my life!

I'm thankful for those who helped me become a better writer by their willingness to read my early efforts and guide me in the process — Rick, Denny, Terry, and Cara. To Angela Scheff, my editor and the one who was willing to take a chance on me and my idea, thank you. You are so good at what you do! To Scott Heagle and the rest of the team at Zondervan, thank you for your encouragement and guidance throughout this process.

ACKNOWLEDGMENTS

I am enormously grateful to those whose stories are included in this book — some of whom I've mentioned by name and some of whom I've shared about without mentioning their names or have given them new names to protect their privacy. I'm also grateful to all who have befriended me, even when they disagreed with, disregarded, or disliked me.

Special thanks to Scott Hodge, Larry Boatright, Mike Jones, and The Orchard Commuity in Aurora, Illinois, for coming up with the title "Not Like Me" for their sermon series and for taking their small groups through the original edition of this book.

It's been a huge privilege to interact with so many amazing people over the years in California, Texas, and Seattle. A special thanks to the wonderful teachers, leaders, and people who influenced my life at The Anchor, North Waco, Emmanuel, Shady Oaks, Baylor, Trinity High, Bacon Heights, and Golden Gate Seminary (Northwest). For those in my life who are a part of Bethel (Leadership Vision and DMin cohorts), Awaken, the Mosaic Alliance, and my friends around the planet I've met over the years, thank you. Thanks to my friends and neighbors in Alhambra with Little League baseball and on Front Street — especially Alex, Jennifer, Samantha, Isabella, Isai, Valerie, Isaiah, Sebastian, John, Bea, and Gabriel's family. Thanks for teaching us how neighbors ought to live together.

Finally, I'm grateful for my extended family. They have loved me even when I fought with my brother, grew long hair, voiced my opinions, and moved far away. Thanks for infusing within my DNA a love for God, a love for family, and a love for sharing stories. Thanks to Grandma, Dema, the Bryants, the Snarrs, the Kohlers, the Pedersons, the Murphys, the Ellises, the Gaddys, the Mathenys, and the Irbys. I would like to especially thank my mom, dad, and brother, Scott, for showing me how to love, how to work, and how to have fun.

Now that I hear the music playing a bit louder, I must quote Paul, who summarizes how I want to live my life:

> I have been crucified with Christ and I no longer live, but Christ lives in me. The life I now live in the body, I live by faith in the Son of God, who loved me and gave himself for me.
>
> **Galatians 2:20**

> I consider my life worth nothing to me; my only aim is to finish the race and complete the task the Lord Jesus has given me — the task of testifying to the good news of God's grace.
>
> **Acts 20:24**

Thank you, Jesus, for loving me and changing me. May these statements be true of me more and more each day.

INTERACTIVE QUESTIONS

CHAPTER 1: CURRYING FAVOR

1. What are some examples of moments when you were able to "become all things" to someone around you in order to demonstrate Christ's love?

2. How would those who don't know Christ but who know you describe you?

3. Have you ever been hurt in your relationship with God because of the actions of a person who claimed to be a Christian? What happened? What helped you overcome that pain?

4. Have you ever inadvertently or even purposely hurt someone's relationship with God? What happened? How have you been able to repair that damage?

5. Who are the people for whom you have played "matchmaker" by connecting them to Christ?

CHAPTER 2: BOUNCE HOUSES IN THE NEIGHBORHOOD

1. What are some of your favorite neighborhood memories?

2. How many of your current neighbors do you know by name?

3. How many of your neighbors would you consider to be your friends (more than simply acquaintances)?

4. What keeps people from engaging in new relationships?

5. What are some practical ways you can bring light into your neighborhood?

CHAPTER 3: PEPPERMINT-FILLED PIÑATAS

1. What elements are included in a great party?

2. Who are the people in your life who need a party?

3. Who are the people within your *oikos* (family, neighbors, coworkers, or friends) who do not yet know Christ? How can you serve them?

4. Who are some *xenoi* (strangers) you can get to know? How can you serve them?

CHAPTER 4: A FELLOWSHIP OF FREAKS

1. What cause in your life brought you together with others you may not have known?

2. What other causes in your life have helped you connect with others?

3. Which hobbies or activities do you want to pursue in order to develop new friendships?

4. How have you been able to grow to be more personally connected to the cause of Christ?

CHAPTER 5: UNCIVIL WAR

1. What are some of your spiritual gifts or strengths? What are some of the spiritual gifts or strengths of those closest to you (at home, work, school, and church)?

2. How do you approach conflict in your life?

3. Do you have something against someone, or does anyone have something against you? If so, what is your plan for resolving these conflicts?

4. Do you have any "enemies"? If so, what have you done to bring peace, or what could you do?

CHAPTER 6: WHITE MEN CAN JUMP (JUST NOT AS HIGH)

1. Have you ever made a decision based on a stereotype? Share some examples.

2. How have you been the victim of stereotyping?

3. What new things can you do to show the world you represent God's love for all people?

4. How can you move beyond racial reconciliation and live a life reconciled to others? What sacrifices would your church or business need to make in order to move toward ethnic diversity?

5. Do you have neighbors, coworkers, or family members from different ethnic backgrounds? How can you reach out to love them, serve them, and learn from them?

CHAPTER 7: THE UNTOUCHABLES

1. What are the socioeconomic demographics of your city?

2. What are the local churches, nonprofit organizations, and government agencies doing to help those in need?

3. What are some practical ways you, your family, your small group, or your church can serve those in need?

4. Who are others your community often overlooks?

5. How can you serve those who are considered "untouchables" in your area?

CHAPTER 8: COMPASSIONATE CONSERVATIVES AND LOVING LIBERALS

1. Do you have friends with whom you disagree politically? Are these friends followers of Christ? Are they non-Christians?

2. How close are you willing to get to these friends? How close is too close, or is that even possible?

3. How can you more actively serve and love others with whom you disagree without compromising your convictions?

4. When is it appropriate to partner with others who do not agree with us?

CHAPTER 9: LOTS OF SEX IN THE CITY

1. Do you have friends with whom you disagree morally? Are these friends followers of Christ? Are they non-Christians?

2. How close are you willing to get to these friends? How close is too close, or is that even possible?

3. What can you do to convey Christ's love to those you know who are living a homosexual lifestyle? What about those who are active sexually outside of marriage?

4. How should you respond to someone who claims to follow Christ yet would be included on Paul's list in 1 Corinthians 6:9 – 10 (thief, slanderer, homosexual, etc.)?

5. When you are struggling, where can you go for help or healing?

CHAPTER 10: THE MOSQUE NEXT DOOR

1. Do you have any friendships with people from other religious backgrounds? If so, how have you been able to serve and love them?

2. Who are the "persons of peace" in your life?

3. How can you catalyze new relationships with those around you?

4. What is your mission field?

5. How are you supporting those who are serving the nations abroad?

6. How can you serve the nations abroad?

NOTES

Introduction: The Art of Woo

1. Sun Tzu, *The Art of War*, trans. Stephen Kaufmann (Boston: Tuttle, 1996).

2. Robert Greene, *The Art of Seduction* (New York: Viking, 1998).

3. Read more about "woo" in Awaken's *Start with Talent, Finish with Strength* (available at www.awakenhumanity.org) or in any of the numerous books written or cowritten by Donald O. Clifton.

Chapter 2: Bounce Houses in the Neighborhood

1. Robert Fishman, *Bourgeois Utopias* (New York: Basic Books, 1989), 58.

2. Harvie Conn and Manuel Ortiz, *Urban Ministry* (Downers Grove, Ill.: InterVarsity, 2001), 69.

Chapter 3: Peppermint-Filled Piñatas

1. At Mosaic we emphasize the importance of having healthy relationships. Our pastor, Erwin McManus, speaks annually on this topic of a "party theology." Drawing applications from the life of Matthew, he challenges us to throw more parties to connect people to Jesus.

Chapter 6: White Men Can Jump (Just Not as High)

1. "Mujahideen" refers, literally, to "those who wage jihad." According to Merriam-Webster, the mujahideen are "Islamic guerilla fighters esp. in the Middle East."

Chapter 7: The Untouchables

1. See Harvie Conn and Manuel Ortiz, *Urban Ministry* (Downers Grove, Ill.: Inter-Varsity, 2001), 120.

2. Conn and Ortiz, *Urban Ministry*, 22, 64.

3. Cited by Keith Phillips, president of World Impact (www.worldimpact.org).

4. Mary Glenn, Alhambra city catalyst, "Kingdom Causes" (www.kingdomcauses .org).

5. Jeffrey D. Sachs, *The End of Poverty* (New York: Penguin, 2005), 347, 368.

Chapter 8: Compassionate Conservatives and Loving Liberals

1. Leslie Berestein, "Highway Safety Sign Becomes Running Story on Immigration," *San Diego Tribune*, April 10, 2005. Can be viewed online at *SignOnSanDiego.com: www.signonsandiego.com/uniontrib/20050410/news_1n10signs.html* (October 17, 2006).

2. Thomas Sowell, *Race and Culture* (New York: Basic Books, 1995), 33.

3. Jim Wallis, *God's Politics* (San Francisco: HarperSanFrancisco, 2005).

4. "Interview with Howard Dean," *The Daily Show with Jon Stewart*, June 23, 2005.

5. Cited in Doris Kearns Goodwin, *Team of Rivals* (New York: Simon & Schuster, 2005), 206.

Awaken is a collaboration between a team of dreamers and innovators who unleash personal and organizational creativity. Awaken serves humanity through the arts, films, music, books, online dialogue, conferences, the Mosaic Alliance, and humanitarian projects. Awaken emerges out of the unique ministry of Mosaic and reflects Mosaic's commitment to entrepreneurship, activism, innovation, authenticity, and creativity.

AWAKEN

www.awaken.org   Awaken Humanity

www.mosaicalliance.com   Create the Future

Free Online Resources at
www.zondervan.com

Daily Bible Verses and Devotions: Enrich your life with daily Bible verses or devotions that help you start every morning focused on God. Visit www.zondervan.com/newsletters.

Free Email Publications: Sign up for newsletters on Christian living, academic resources, church ministry, fiction, children's resources, and more. Visit www.zondervan.com/newsletters.

Zondervan Bible Search: Find and compare Bible passages in a variety of translations at www.zondervanbiblesearch.com.

Other Benefits: Register yourself to receive online benefits like coupons and special offers, or to participate in research.

CPSIA information can be obtained at www.ICGtesting.com
Printed in the USA
LVOW08s1006010316

477202LV00003B/4/P